High Interest
Easy Reading

High Interest Easy Reading

For Junior and Senior
High School Students

Fourth Edition

Hugh Agee, Chair,
and the Committee to Revise
High Interest—Easy Reading
of the National Council of Teachers of English

National Council of Teachers of English
1111 Kenyon Road, Urbana, Illinois 61801

Book Design: Tom Kovacs for TGK Design, interior; Vicki Martin, cover

NCTE Stock Number 20954

Library of Congress Cataloging in Publication Data

National Council of Teachers of English.   Committee
        to Revise High Interest-Easy Reading.
        High interest easy reading.

        Summary: Annotates approximately 400 recommended books of interest to the reluctant high school reader, arranged alphabetically within eighteen categories including adventure, trivia, careers, fantasy, and history.
        1. High interest-low vocabulary books—Bibliography.
[1. High interest-low vocabulary books—Bibliography.
2. Bibliography—Best books]   I. Agee, Hugh, 1933-   .
II. Title.
Z1039.S5N4   1984   028.5'35   83-25107

ISBN 0-8141-2095-4

Contents

Introduction to the Reader

This book's for you. A group of teachers has looked at hundreds of books published in the last few years and selected those we think will most interest you as an active young person. We realize there are many demands on your time and that you often put books and reading aside in favor of, say, watching television. Yet, whether you find yourself needing a book for a school assignment or simply for discovering more about a person or topic that interests you, you may not always know how to find just that right book. We hope this list of recently published books will be of help to you.

The books in this booklist are divided into eighteen categories, ranging from Adventure to Trivia and including such different topics as Careers, Fantasy, History: Fact and Fiction, and the Supernatural. Within each category, books are arranged alphabetically by the author's last name. After the author's name are the title of the book, the name of the publishing company, and the publication date. Last comes the International Standard Book Number (ISBN), which will aid your teacher or librarian in ordering a book from the publisher. A brief description is included for each book to introduce you to the main theme or main character. A typical entry reads this way:

Smith, Pauline C. **Brush Fire!** Hiway Books, 1979. ISBN 0-664-32639-0.

Johnny, a high school junior, is taking care of the Millers' home while they are away for the summer. Then a motorcycle gang starts a brush fire that threatens the house, and Johnny must try to control the fire. Fiction.

Following the section of Trivia books are descriptions of fourteen series of books on such topics as adventure, mystery, and science. If you enjoy one book in a series, you may want to read some of the other titles as well.

At the end of this book are a list of publishers and their addresses and two indexes—one arranged by author and the other by book title.

Many of the books have been selected on the advice of other high school students. We hope you have the same positive reactions as these students had. Remember that a book works no magic on its own. Only when you, the reader, pick it up and become involved with it does it come alive. Then it has the power to entertain, to inspire, to inform, to persuade. It's up to you to give a book a chance.

Again, this book's for you. May it bring you into the habit of reading and enjoying books as an important part of your life.

High Interest
Easy Reading

Book Descriptions

ADVENTURE

Boehm, Bruce, and Janet Winn. **Connecticut Low.** Houghton Mifflin Co., 1980. ISBN 0-395-29518-1.

A fourteen-year-old boy finds happiness as he explores the Connecticut River and discovers a secret friend who teaches him about nature. When a flood comes, this same river brings death to the boy's friend. But it also brings the boy and his father closer together as the boy shows bravery in rescuing people during the flood. Fiction.

Breckler, Rosemary. **Where Are the Twins?** Hiway Books, 1979. ISBN 0-664-32651-X.

While searching for twins who disappeared during a rainstorm and mudslides, two teenagers help their community in other ways as well. Everyone shows appreciation at a special assembly, and the teenagers become official Police Cadets. Fiction.

Fife, Dale. **Destination Unknown.** Unicorn Books, 1981. ISBN 0-525-28624-1.

Twelve-year-old Jon Lunde is separated from his parents and stranded on the Faeroe Islands when the Nazis occupy his native Norway in the 1940s. So he stows away on a fishing boat. But Jon soon realizes the boat is being forced to cross the Atlantic to Canada because of the trouble with the Nazis in the North Atlantic. Fiction.

Forman, James D. **Call Back Yesterday.** Signet Vista Books, 1982. ISBN 0-684-17168-6.

Cindy is visiting her parents in Saudi Arabia, where her father works in the American embassy. Her involvement with two young men leads to the bombing of the embassy. Cindy, as the only survivor, now has to recall that night of horror for officials who are trying to prevent a world crisis. Fiction.

Kherdian, David. **It Started with Old Man Bean.** Greenwillow Books, 1980. ISBN 0-688-80247-8.

Two responsible, clever young men get the money to pay for a camping trip. When a storm comes, Ted and Joe struggle to get home, even though they take a risk that could be fatal. Fiction.

Love, Sandra. **Dive for the Sun.** Houghton Mifflin Co., 1982. ISBN 0-395-32864-0.

Bitter and withdrawn after the death of his mother and sister, fifteen-year-old Kris refuses to help his father search for a sunken Spanish treasure ship. Then he has a series of dreams taking him back to a voyage of the ill-fated ship. Kris's attitude changes when he realizes he may hold the key to the treasure's discovery. Fiction.

Lyle, Katie Letcher. **Finders Weepers.** Coward, McCann & Geoghegan, 1982. ISBN 0-698-20556-1.

Thirteen-year-old Lee comes to the mountains to help care for her dying grandmother. While there, she stumbles on the famous Beale treasure, setting off a series of adventures. Fiction.

Marston, Elsa. **The Cliffs of Cairo.** Signet Vista Books, 1982. ISBN 0-451-11530-9.

Sixteen-year-old Tabitha explores historic mosques and ancient buildings while in Cairo, Egypt. Her explorations lead to mazes, danger, art collectors, and cult members. Fiction.

Mazer, Harry. **The Last Mission.** Delacorte Press, 1979. ISBN 0-440-05774-4.

Jack Rabb is fifteen and Jewish. It is 1944 and he desperately wishes to help save the Jewish people in Europe from Hitler. Using his brother's ID card, Jack enlists in the U.S. Air Force and becomes a member of a bomber crew. His experiences are both exciting and horrifying. Fiction.

Packard, Edward. **Deadwood City.** Illus. Paul Granger. Bantam Books, 1980. ISBN 0-553-13994-0.

By playing the role of a cowhand in the Old West, you will make decisions on each page of this book that determine how the story will go on. If you decide to apply for a job riding shotgun, for instance, you will turn to one page. If you decide to inquire about a job at Red Creek Ranch, you turn to another. How everything ends is up to you! Fiction.

Reader, Dennis J. **Coming Back Alive.** Flare Books, 1983. ISBN 0-380-61416-2.

After they are tragically separated from their parents, two young friends run away to live in the mountains of northern California. There they try to survive on their own, living in caves and hunting animals for food and clothing. Fiction.

Roy, Ron. **Avalanche!** Illus. Robert MacLean. Unicorn Books, 1981. ISBN 0-525-26060-9.

Two brothers are separated when Tony, the older brother, suddenly leaves town. Six years later, his brother Scott is sent to visit Tony while their parents make plans for a divorce. Being together once more brings them closer as brothers, but their ski trip is interrupted by an avalanche that separates the two once again. Fiction.

Roy, Ron. **Nightmare Island.** Illus. Robert MacLean. Unicorn Books, 1981. ISBN 0-525-35905-2.

Little Island becomes Nightmare Island when two brothers on a camping trip throw a burning bush into the water—and the ocean bursts into flame. Both brothers show courage and faith as they search for a way to escape from the island. Fiction.

Skármeta, Antonio (translator Hortense Carpentier). **Chileno!** William Morrow & Co., 1979. ISBN 0-688-22213-7 (ISBN 0-688-32213-1, library binding).

A fourteen-year-old leaves his native country of Chile to grow up in Berlin, Germany. Here he encounters new friends and tries to cope with the demands of his parents. He also shows courage when he has to fight the toughest guy in town to protect his girlfriend. Fiction.

Smith, Pauline C. **Brush Fire!** Hiway Books, 1979. ISBN 0-664-32639-0.

Johnny, a high school junior, is taking care of the Millers' home while they are away for the summer. Then a motorcycle gang starts a brush fire that threatens the house, and Johnny must try to control the fire. Fiction.

Sobol, Donald J. **Disaster.** Archway Paperbacks, 1979. ISBN 0-671-43133-1.

Here are true stories of people caught up in every kind of disaster you can imagine. There are tales of horror, sadness, and courage. Nonfiction.

Stone, Nancy Y. **Dune Shadow.** Houghton Mifflin Co., 1980. ISBN 0-395-29744-3.

A Michigan village becomes a ghost town in the nineteenth century when families flee an approaching sand dune. Soon the only people left are thirteen-year-old Serena, her grandmother, and her friend Jody. When Granny becomes weaker, Serena decides to take charge and find shelter elsewhere. Fiction.

Wartski, Maureen Crane. **The Lake Is on Fire.** Signet Vista Books, 1982. ISBN 0-451-11942-8.

A blind fifteen-year-old boy and a strange, half-savage dog are trapped together during a storm. Together for more than twenty-four hours, they save each other again and again while they wait to be rescued. Fiction.

Zaring, Jane. **Sharkes in the North Woods, or Nish Na Bosh Na Is Nicer Now.** Houghton Mifflin Co., 1982. ISBN 0-395-32271-5.

The Sharkes family run a summer camp for children—and plan to get rich by holding the children for ransom. But four of the campers escape and try to foil the Sharkes' evil plans. Fiction.

ANIMALS

Aaron, Chester. **Duchess.** J. B. Lippincott Co., 1982. ISBN 0-397-31947-9 (ISBN 0-397-31948-7, library binding).

Thirteen-year-old Marty goes to live on his uncle's sheep ranch to avoid going to jail. He decides to run away, but then he finds a starving dog in his uncle's shed. Marty rescues and trains the dog, and learns about friendship and responsibility. Fiction.

Adler, C. S. **Shelter on Blue Barns Road.** Macmillan Publishing Co., 1981. ISBN 0-02-700280-2. Signet Vista Books, 1982 (paperback). ISBN 0-451-11438-8.

Thirteen-year-old Betsy's family moves from Brooklyn, New York, to a small town. There she befriends a vicious Doberman at the nearby animal shelter. But her efforts to adopt the dog nearly lead to disaster. Fiction.

Bunting, Eve. **The Great White Shark.** Julian Messner, 1982. ISBN 0-671-44004-7.

Where do the great white sharks come from? How do they live and breed? What can you do to avoid being attacked by one of these sharks? This book provides interesting answers to these and many other questions through its text and photographs. Nonfiction.

Burrud, Bill (with Allen Rich). **Bill Burrud's Animal Quiz.** Tempo Books, 1979. ISBN 0-448-17079-5.

Do monkeys blush? Are fish silent when they are underwater? Here are fifty-eight short quizzes about the animal kingdom to challenge the reader. The answers that follow each quiz give information about animals of every kind. Photographs. Nonfiction.

Clarkson, Ewan. **Wolves.** Raintree Childrens Books, 1980. ISBN 0-8172-1089-X.

This story of the first year in the life of a wolf cub reveals that wolves are not vicious beasts that eat human flesh, as many people think. The book contains many color photos of wolves in their natural surroundings. Also in this series are *Whales and Dolphins* (by Terence Wise), *Tigers* (by Cathy Kilpatrick), and eleven other book on animals. Nonfiction.

Clemens, Virginia Phelps. **SuperAnimals and Their Unusual Careers.** Westminster Press, 1979. ISBN 0-664-32649-8.

Some are famous, others are not, but all the animals presented in this book are exceptional in one way or another. There are German shepherds that sniff for explosives, a wrestling bear, and assorted cats, dogs, and horses trained for television advertisements. The behind-the-scenes information about these animals is even more fascinating than their performances. Nonfiction.

Cohen, Daniel. **Bigfoot: America's Number One Monster.** Archway Paperbacks, 1982. ISBN 0-671-42919-7.

What is Bigfoot? Dozens of encounters with this creature are reported here. From these stories, maybe you can decide whether it is an ape, a primitive human form, a creature from outer space, a hoax, or a myth. Nonfiction.

Dinneen, Betty. **The Family Howl.** Illus. Stefen Bernath. Macmillan Publishing Co., 1981. ISBN 0-02-732150-9.

Two silver-backed jackals, Russett and Silverback, raise their four pups in the Nairobi National Park in Africa. They must rely on speed, patience, and cunning to compete for food and escape their enemies. Nonfiction.

Hall, Lynn. **The Horse Trader.** Charles Scribner's Sons, 1981. ISBN 0-684-16852-9.

Karen, fifteen and fatherless, is grateful when Harley Williams, the local horse trader, finds a mare that she can afford to buy. But after the first time she rides her horse, she begins to wonder if her friend Harley isn't also a con man. Fiction.

Harris, Mark Jonathan. **The Last Run.** Lothrop, Lee & Shepard Books, 1981. ISBN 0-688-00634-5 (ISBN 0-688-00635-3, library binding).

Fourteen-year-old Lyle is restless and unhappy. He lives in a small Nevada town and pumps gas at his father's garage. But Lyle has a dream. He hopes to capture a horse for himself when he goes on a roundup with his grandfather, who is famous for his skill at capturing horses. Fiction.

Meyers, Susan. **Pearson: A Harbor Seal Pup.** Photographs by Ilka Hartmann. E. P. Dutton, 1980. ISBN 0-525-36845-0.

When a woman finds a half-starved orphan seal pup on a California beach, she takes him to the California Marine Mammal Center. There, marine experts work to save the pup's life. Many photographs illustrate the seal's growth and development. Nonfiction.

Morey, Walt. **The Lemon Meringue Dog.** E. P. Dutton, 1980. ISBN 0-525-33455-6.

When Chris's search dog, Mike, sniffs out a lemon meringue pie instead of heroin, both are thrown off the Coast Guard's drug detection team. But when Chris takes a job as a night guard at the post office, Mike's good nose nearly gets them killed. Fiction.

Patent, Dorothy Hinshaw. **Horses and Their Wild Relatives.** Holiday House, 1981. ISBN 0-8234-0383-1.

The author traces the family history of horses back sixty million years to show how each family branch has adapted to its surroundings. The book includes information about herd life among wild horses and discussions of how horses are related to zebras, jackasses, tapirs, and rhinos. Nonfiction.

Patent, Dorothy Hinshaw. **Hunters and the Hunted: Surviving in the Animal World.** Holiday House, 1981. ISBN 0-8234-0386-6.

How lions hunt antelopes, how spiders capture moths, how moths use sound to escape bats—these and other accounts in this book show how, through the ages, both the hunters and the hunted are always improving the way they capture their prey or escape being a victim. Many photographs are included to illustrate this battle for survival between animals. Nonfiction.

Pinkwater, Jill, and D. Manus Pinkwater. **Superpuppy: How to Choose, Raise, and Train the Best Possible Dog for You.** Illus. Jill Pinkwater. Clarion Books, 1982. ISBN 0-89919-084-7.

They all look so cute in the pet store windows. But, what do you do with your dog once you get it home? This book will tell you how to choose, care for, and train a puppy. It will also help you understand a dog's feelings and personality. Nonfiction.

Rounds, Glen. **Blind Outlaw.** Illus. by author. Holiday House, 1980. ISBN 0-8234-0423-4.

A boy who cannot speak uses patience and skill to tame a blind outlaw horse. But the horse escapes in panic when a prairie fire approaches the ranch. The boy sets out across the prairie, knowing that he will have to regain the horse's trust—if he can find him. Fiction.

Steneman, Shep. **Garfield: The Complete Cat Book.** Illus. Jim Davis. Random House, 1981. ISBN 0-394-84893-4.

Here is a goldmine of information and entertainment for cat lovers. You will find cats in history, cat names, cat proverbs, true stories and myths about cats, and dozens of cartoons featuring Garfield. Photographs. Nonfiction.

Stoneley, Jack. **Scruffy.** Archway Paperbacks, 1981. ISBN 0-671-41096-2.

Scruffy is an orphan mongrel puppy who roams the city. During his adventures, he deals with human friends and enemies, finds romance with a bullterrier, and faces death at the animal shelter. Originally published as *The Tuesday Dog*. Fiction.

Van Steenwyk, Elizabeth. **Quarter Horse Winner.** Illus. Susan Mohn. Albert Whitman & Co., 1980. ISBN 0-8075-6707-8.

Thirteen-year-old Holly is training her horse Buddy for a new event. While she does this, Holly learns some lessons about self-confidence from a shy friend, a lonely cousin, and a nervous Buddy. Fiction.

Weaver, John L. **Grizzly Bears.** Skylight Books, 1982. ISBN 0-396-08084-7.

The first fifteen months in the lives of three grizzly bear cubs are covered in this book. A wildlife biologist follows the bears around the Rockies to discover how they survive from day to day in their natural environment. Photographs. Nonfiction.

BIOGRAPHY

Aaseng, Nathan. **Eric Heiden: Winner in Gold.** Lerner Publications Co., 1980. ISBN 0-8225-0481-2.

Eric Heiden won five gold medals in speed skating at the 1980 Winter Olympics at Lake Placid. This brief biography covers all aspects of his successful speed skating career and the training necessary to achieve that success. The text is illustrated with many action photographs. Nonfiction.

Aaseng, Nathan. **Pete Rose: Baseball's Charlie Hustle.** Lerner Publications Co., 1981. ISBN 0-8225-0480-4.

Now in his forties, Pete Rose has had a long and successful career in professional baseball. He has had ten seasons with more than 200 hits and over 3,000 lifetime hits. This book shows how much hard work and determination Rose has put into his baseball career. Nonfiction.

Alderman, Clifford Lindsey. **Annie Oakley and the World of Her Time.** Macmillan Publishing Co., 1979. ISBN 0-02-700270-5.

As a child of a poor family, Annie Oakley (1860–1926) became a circus sharpshooter in order to put food on the table. Soon shooting became a lifelong career for Annie as she joined Buffalo Bill's Wild West Show and toured the United States and the world showing off her skills. Nonfiction.

Blassingame, Wyatt. **Thor Heyerdahl: Viking Scientist.** Elsevier/Nelson Books, 1979. ISBN 0-525-66626-5.

Thor Heyerdahl believed that the Pacific islanders and the pre-Columbian Indians of South America shared a common culture. The only way to prove this theory was to build a balsa raft and sail it from Peru to Polynesia in 1947. The voyage was daring and dangerous, but Heyerdahl was successful. Nonfiction.

Brown, Marion Marsh. **Homeward the Arrow's Flight.** Abingdon Press, 1980. ISBN 0-687-17300-0.

Susan La Flesche was the first American Indian woman to become a doctor. Reaching her goal took courage, brains, and determination. When she got her medical degree, La Flesche returned to her reservation in Nebraska in the 1800s to care for her people, the Omaha Indians. Nonfiction.

Burchard, S. H. **Sports Star: Elvin Hayes.** Harcourt Brace Jovanovich, 1980. ISBN 0-15-278018-1 (ISBN 0-15-684828-7, paperback).

As a young man, Elvin Hayes left the poverty and prejudice of his hometown in the 1960s to play college and pro basketball. But even as a sports star, Hayes found success mixed with prejudice, failure, and disappointment. He finally learned to deal with his problems by turning to God. Photographs. Nonfiction.

Davidson, Margaret. **The Golda Meir Story.** Rev. ed. Charles Scribner's Sons, 1981. ISBN 0-684-16877-4.

Golda Meir was a pioneer in the founding of Israel as a Jewish homeland in 1948. There she later was elected prime minister. This book includes details of her life as well as her political views. Nonfiction.

Drucker, Malka (with George Foster). **The George Foster Story.** Holiday House, 1980. ISBN 0-8234-0413-7.

This book gives an inspiring account of George Foster's baseball career and his philosophy of the game. Foster was born in Tuscaloosa, Alabama, in 1948. Later he moved to California and started to fulfill his dream of becoming a baseball star. But the road to success was filled with sacrifice and hard work. Nonfiction.

Gutman, Bill. **Baseball Belters: Jackson, Schmidt, Parker, Brett.** Tempo Books, 1981. ISBN 0-448-17375-5.

This book describes the interesting stories behind the careers of four baseball stars, from their start in the game to the present. There is also a section of statistics showing the tremendous talents each man possesses. Nonfiction.

Libby, Bill. **Joe Louis: The Brown Bomber.** Lothrop, Lee & Shepard Books, 1980. ISBN 0-688-41968-2.

Joe Louis, known as the "Brown Bomber" of the 1930s, may have been the greatest heavyweight champion in boxing history. This book tells the story of the man who held that title longer than any other man—more than eleven years—and who defended it more often. Nonfiction.

Libby, Bill. **The Reggie Jackson Story.** Lothrop, Lee & Shepard Books, 1979. ISBN 0-688-41889-9.

Who is six feet tall, weighs 200 pounds, and has the speed of a sprinter? Reggie Jackson, also known as "Mr. October." Here is the story of Jackson's life and career as one of baseball's most exciting and talked-about superstars. Nonfiction.

Liss, Howard. **Picture Story of Dave Winfield.** Julian Messner, 1982. ISBN 0-671-44271-6.

Dave Winfield is shown here, through career statistics and stories of his family life, as both a great baseball player and an admirable man. Nonfiction.

Page, N. H. **Bobby Orr—Number Four.** Laurel-Leaf Books, 1982. ISBN 0-440-90628-8.

Bobby Orr is one of the greatest players in National Hockey League history. This book takes the reader through Orr's career to one of his greatest triumphs—having his Boston Bruins' jersey (number 4) retired. Nonfiction.

Shyne, Kevin. **The Man Who Dropped from the Sky.** Julian Messner, 1982. ISBN 0-671-44164-7.

Roger Reynolds was seventeen years old when he took his first jump from an airplane in 1980. He found a challenge in parachute jumping—until an unfortunate accident put him in a hospital for over a year. But with stubborn determination, Reynolds got back on his feet, ran in the Boston Marathon, and even took up skydiving again. Nonfiction.

Sullivan, George. **Superstars of Women's Track.** Dodd, Mead & Co., 1981. ISBN 0-396-07989-X.

Some of the most exciting performances ever by female athletes happened in track and field in the 1970s. Based on personal interviews, these stories of Mary Decker, Grete Waitz, Evelyn Ashford, Madeline Manning, Julie Shea, and Candy Young all show how hard work, determination, and courage are needed for sports success. Photographs. Nonfiction.

CAREERS

Anderson, David. **The Piano Makers.** Photographs by author. Pantheon Books, 1982. ISBN 0-394-85353-9 (ISBN 0-394-95353-3, library binding).

We have all heard a piano. But have you ever wondered how a piano is put together to make those sounds? This book gives a behind-the-scenes look at the people and skills that go into making a grand piano. Nonfiction.

Cole, Sheila. **Working Kids on Working.** Photographs by Victoria Beller-Smith. Lothrop, Lee & Shepard Books, 1980. ISBN 0-688-41959-3.

What kinds of work do kids do? Some young people work at fast-food places to gain independence. Some help their families by working outside as well as inside the home, caring for parents or younger family members. Some prepare for future careers, learning such things as dance and farming. This book contains interviews with kids doing all kinds of work for all kinds of reasons. Nonfiction.

Dean, Karen Strickler. **Between Dances: Maggie Adams' Eighteenth Summer.** Flare Books, 1980. ISBN 0-380-80200-7.

In this sequel to *Maggie Adams, Dancer,* Maggie is of age. Finally, her father accepts the fact that his daughter will be a dancer and begins to support her. Maggie becomes engaged, but then she must decide between her dancing career and marriage. Fiction.

Dean, Karen Strickler. **Maggie Adams, Dancer.** Flare Books, 1980. ISBN 0-380-75366-9.

This book features a young girl, Maggie, who is determined to get to the top as a ballet dancer. Regardless of such obstacles as age, accidents, losing her boyfriend, having biased judges, and other pressures, Maggie continues to have hope. Fiction.

Gilbert, Sara. **Ready, Set, Go: How to Find a Career That's Right for You.** Four Winds Press, 1979. ISBN 0-590-07566-7.

What kinds of jobs are right for you? This book offers information to help you decide on a career, a decision involving such important questions as: Who am I? What am I good at? What do

I want out of life? It also describes many different types of jobs. Nonfiction.

Gutman, Bill. **Women Who Work with Animals.** Dodd, Mead & Co., 1982. ISBN 0-396-08035-9.

A child's interest in animals can lead to a career with animals. Here are the stories of six women—a zookeeper, a dog trainer, a veterinarian, a racehorse trainer, a dolphin trainer, and a television personality—whose love of animals led them into careers traditionally held by men. Photographs. Nonfiction.

CARS AND OTHER MACHINES

Berliner, Don. **Flying-Model Airplanes.** Lerner Publications Co., 1982. ISBN 0-8225-1449-9.

Until the time you can fly an actual plane, have you ever thought of flying model airplanes? Here is an overview of the hobby of model airplanes that fly. Everything from rubber-band models to operating jets is discussed, including free-flight, radio-controlled, and control-line models. Nonfiction.

Berliner, Don. **Personal Airplanes.** Lerner Publications Co., 1982. ISBN 0-8225-0447-2.

This book provides information about small airplanes: how they work, what they are used for, how to get a license to fly them. Nonfiction.

Clark, James. **Cars.** Illus. John Bailey and John Dyess. Raintree Publishers, 1981. ISBN 0-8172-1405-4.

Can you tell the difference between a distributor and carburetor? Here is a complete, illustrated description of how cars work: braking and electrical systems, engines, and transmissions. You will also learn about unusual models and about fuels other than gasoline. Nonfiction.

Dolan, Edward F., Jr. **Bicycle Touring and Camping.** Photographs by Jay Irving. Julian Messner, 1982. ISBN 0-671-42876-4.

For your next vacation, why not forget cars, planes, and boats and use your bike to travel. With careful preparation, bicycle touring can be an enjoyable and safe way to travel. Whether you are a beginner or an experienced cyclist, the useful tips in this book will make your trip more enjoyable. Nonfiction.

Hallman, Ruth. **Midnight Wheels.** Hiway Books, 1979. ISBN 0-664-32650-1.

Nineteen-year-old Angie Duncan is a first-rate mechanic at Martin's Garage. She is also a karate student, working to keep in top shape both physically and mentally. Then a warning from a friend and some suspicions of her own lead Angie to investigate some unusual events. What she learns puts her in great danger. Fiction.

Hallman, Ruth. **Rescue Chopper.** Hiway Books, 1980. ISBN 0-664-32667-6. Laurel-Leaf Books, 1981 (paperback). ISBN 0-440-97398-8.

Commander Scott Keane and his crew carry out daring rescues in their Coast Guard *HH3F 1027* search and rescue helicopter. Fiction.

Kleiner, Art. **Robots.** Illus. Jerry Scott. Raintree Publishers, 1981. ISBN 0-8172-1401-1.

Robots are here to stay, so why not get to know them? Through diagrams and illustrations, this book describes the operation of robots and discusses the development, uses, and future of these machines. Nonfiction.

Lindblom, Steven. **The Fantastic Bicycles Book.** Houghton Mifflin Co., 1979. ISBN 0-395-28481-3 (ISBN 0-395-28432-1, paperback).

Do you like to work on bicycles? This book has explanations of how to build and maintain a variety of custom bikes from salvage parts: BMX, ski, racing, tandem, water, and other styles. Detailed drawings make the instructions clear. Nonfiction.

Marston, Hope Irvin. **Machines on the Farm.** Dodd, Mead & Co., 1982. ISBN 0-396-08070-7.

Old MacDonald would probably never have been successful on a modern farm unless he learned about the latest farm equipment. A vast array of farm machines is described and illustrated in this book—tractors, balers, combines, cultivators, sprayers, planters, grain drills, harrows, and many others. Nonfiction.

Oliver, Carl R., compiler. **Plane Talk: Aviators' and Astronauts' Own Stories.** Houghton Mifflin Co., 1980. ISBN 0-395-29743-5.

These stories come straight from the people who have made aviation history. Learn about the sensation of flying experimental jets high above the atmosphere. Follow the equally dangerous feats of the early pilots, who had to invent everything from instruments to seat belts. Photographs. Nonfiction.

Olney, Ross R. **Modern Drag Racing Superstars.** Dodd, Mead & Co., 1981. ISBN 0-396-07925-3.

Here are the stories of six top professional drag racers: Bob Glidden, Tom McEwen, Don Prudhomme, Don Garlits, Gary Beck, and Shirley Muldowney, who is recognized everywhere as the best in the sport. Photographs show the excitement of professional drag racing. Nonfiction.

Wenzel, Celeste Piano. **The Crazy Custom Car Book.** Julian Messner, 1982. ISBN 0-671-43777-1.

Some people are never satisfied with the cars they get from the factory. They have to make them different and even outrageous. The first half of this book traces the history of custom cars from the beginning of automobile manufacturing to the present. The second half has photographs and descriptions of various crazy cars from the Bathtub Buggy to the Li'l Stinker, a converted manure spreader! Nonfiction.

ETHNIC EXPERIENCES

Coates, Belle. **Mak.** Parnassus Press, 1981. ISBN 0-395-31603-0.

Mak, an Indian teenager on a Montana reservation, works as guide to a scientist hunting for fossils. Now he must cope with the conflict within himself between the scientific search for fossils and his Indian love of the land. Fiction.

Engel, Beth Bland. **Big Words.** Lodestar Books, 1982. ISBN 0-525-66779-2.

Black high school senior Will Brown has been accused of murdering a white woman in a southern town in the 1960s. Twelve-year-old Sandy Cason believes he is innocent and decides to hide Will until the real murderer is found. Fiction.

Mangurian, David. **Children of the Incas.** Four Winds Press, 1979. ISBN 0-590-07500-4.

Thirteen-year-old Modesto talks about daily life in Coata, Peru, where descendants of the once-mighty Incas now struggle for survival. Photographs help to make Modesto's story come alive. Nonfiction.

Myers, Walter Dean. **Won't Know Till I Get There.** Viking Press, 1982. ISBN 0-670-77862-1.

Steve and his gang of black friends get into trouble when Steve paints a subway car to show his adopted brother how tough he is. Their punishment is to work in a home for retired but independent senior citizens. Fiction.

Myers, Walter Dean. **The Young Landlords.** Viking Press, 1979. ISBN 0-670-79454-6. Flare Books, 1980 (paperback). ISBN 0-380-52191-1.

Five teenagers grow up quickly when they become the landlords of a run-down Harlem apartment building. Faced with theft, repair bills, and a shortage of cash, they learn that being landlords is harder than they imagined. Fiction.

Place, Marian T., and Charles G. Preston. **Juan's Eighteen-Wheeler Summer.** Dodd, Mead & Co., 1982. ISBN 0-396-08078-2.

Juan, a Chicano fifth-grader, spends a summer in the produce business. He quickly learns about a trucker's life and responsibilities. As he travels around Southern California with Pete, Juan has a number of new and exciting experiences—he even becomes a hero. Fiction.

Rau, Margaret. **The Minority Peoples of China.** Julian Messner, 1982. ISBN 0-671-41545-X.

Over fifty different ethnic groups live in the mountains or along the borders of the People's Republic of China. This book looks at the life and customs of such groups as the Uygurs, the Kazaks, the Hui, and the Miao. Nonfiction.

FANTASY

Aiken, Joan. **The Stolen Lake.** Delacorte Press, 1981. ISBN 0-440-08317-6.

Twelve-year-old Dido Twite, sailing to England aboard a British man-o'-war, ends up aiding the Queen of New Cumbria, the 1,300-year-old Guinevere. Dido is involved in many exciting adventures as the plot of this mystery, based on the tales of King Arthur, unfolds. Fiction.

Bonham, Frank. **The Forever Formula.** E. P. Dutton, 1979. ISBN 0-525-30025-2.

Evan Clark wakes up in a world different from the one he went to sleep in 180 years before. Those who control this new world think he knows the secret that will keep them alive forever. Evan wonders what they will do to him when he can't give them the formula. Fiction.

Cohen, Daniel. **Creatures from UFO's.** Archway Paperbacks, 1979. ISBN 0-671-29951-4.

Have you ever seen a UFO? This book contains nine stories in which people claim to have seen beings from outer space. Some of the stories are clearly hoaxes. But others just might be true. Illustrations. Nonfiction.

Corbett, Scott. **The Donkey Planet.** Illus. Troy Howell. Unicorn Books, 1979. ISBN 0-525-28825-2.

Two young scientists are sent to the planet Vanaris to collect a sample of its metal. To do this they disguise themselves as a donkey and a twelve-year-old boy. But before they can get the metal and return home, they must defeat the dictator of Vanaris. Fiction.

Fisk, Nicholas. **Escape from Splatterbang.** Macmillan Publishing Co., 1979. ISBN 0-02-735260-9.

Young Mykl is accidentally abandoned on a hostile planet with a gypsy girl and a computer. They discover why the flamers attack, and when Mykl's parents return for him, this knowledge helps them all to escape. Fiction.

Goldberger, Judith M. **The Looking Glass Factor.** E. P. Dutton, 1979. ISBN 0-525-34148-X.

Young Hannah has learned to merge her being with other things, to escape her body. But this experiment may be dangerous, and she has to decide if she can study this rare talent as a scientist, or if she's too inexperienced to deal with it properly. Fiction.

Hoover, H. M. **The Bell Tree.** Viking Press, 1982. ISBN 0-670-15600-0.

On the planet of Tanin, fifteen-year-old Jenny and her father confront powers they do not understand—and also deal with greed, which they understand only too well. As their guide, Eli, helps them explore the ruins of Tanin's ancient civilization, Jenny helps Eli rediscover the joys of human companionship. Fiction.

Hoover, H. M. **The Lost Star.** Viking Press, 1979. ISBN 0-670-44129-5.

Fifteen-year-old Lian, an astrophysicist, has never been allowed to form close human attachments. When she becomes involved in a dig for traces of past civilizations, she meets the Lumpies, gray smiling creatures with a strange secret. As her affection for the Lumpies grows, she finds she has to make some difficult decisions about them. Fiction.

Hoover, H. M. **Return to Earth.** Viking Press, 1980. ISBN 0-670-59593-4. Avon Books, 1981 (paperback). ISBN 0-380-54486-5.

Galen returns to Earth to choose his successor as governor-general of a space colony. He decides fifteen-year-old Samara is the perfect choice. But Samara has problems of her own as the greedy Dolmen tries to get rid of her and increase his own power. Fiction.

Hoover, H. M. **This Time of Darkness.** Viking Press, 1980. ISBN 0-670-50026-7.

Eleven-year-old Amy is too smart and curious for her own good. She must hide her ability to read and think from the Watchers. Then she meets Axel, who claims to be from the outside. Together they set off to climb from their underground world to freedom. Fiction.

Jones, Diana Wynne. **The Homeward Bounders.** Greenwillow Books, 1981. ISBN 0-688-00678-7.

Twelve-year-old Jamie suddenly finds himself being tossed around in space and time. He wanders in and out of worlds, making friends who help him in his efforts to return home. Fiction.

Kennedy, Richard. **The Boxcar at the Center of the Universe.** Illus. Jeff Kronen. Harper & Row, Publishers, 1982. ISBN 0-06-023186-6.

A sixteen-year-old boy in search of his identity meets an old tramp in a boxcar. As he listens to the man's fantastic tales, the boy begins to understand that he, like the old man, is the center of the universe. Fiction.

Lazarus, Keo Felker. **The Gismo.** Illus. Leonard Shortall. Follett Publishing Co., 1981. ISBN 0-695-40145-9.

Two boys find a way to communicate with a being from the planet Monaal. They first meet with this being when they find and return the Gismo, part of the communication system of the Monaal spaceship. First in a three-book series. Fiction.

Lazarus, Keo Felker. **The Gismonauts.** Follett Publishing Co., 1981. ISBN 0-695-41607-3.

In the year 2049, a Boy Scout troop from Earth visits the moon. Two of the scouts discover a space station beneath the moon's surface and have many adventures. Second in a three-book series. Fiction.

Lazarus, Keo Felker. **A Message from Monaal.** Follett Publishing Co., 1981. ISBN 0-695-41606-5.

Monaal invites Earth to join the Intergalactic Federation. But first, Jerry, Chris, and Steve must travel around the world to receive messages from Monaal. Third in a three-book series. Fiction.

Murphy, Shirley Rousseau. **Caves of Fire and Ice.** Flare Books, 1982. ISBN 0-380-58081-0.

Ramad of the Wolves has crossed the barrier of Time, and Skeelie is lonely and lost without his companionship. So Skeelie sets out on an adventurous trek in search of Ramad. Fiction.

Myers, Walter Dean. **Brainstorm.** Photographs by Chuck Freedman. Laurel-Leaf Books, 1979. ISBN 0-440-90788-8.

In the year 2076, the people of Earth are attacked by an unknown force. It steals minds, leaving people as helpless as infants. The crew of the spaceship sent to find this enemy is ordered to try reason first—and then weapons if necessary. But can the crew stop the force before it takes their minds too? Fiction.

Myers, Walter Dean. **The Legend of Tarik.** Viking Press, 1981. ISBN 0-670-42312-2.

Young Tarik sees his West African family destroyed by El Muerte, an evil Spanish warrior. Two wise men save Tarik's life and train him in self-defense and self-discipline. Armed with a magic sword, the Crystal of Truth, and a very special horse, Tarik goes forth to defeat El Muerte. But he finds that killing, even in revenge, is not always satisfying. Fiction.

Parenteau, Shirley. **The Talking Coffins of Cryo-City.** Elsevier/Nelson Books, 1979. ISBN 0-525-66666-4.

Kallie can't understand why the Weather Programmer programs only hot and dry weather, killing her beloved plants. Sure that the machine is malfunctioning, she changes the program to make it rain. For this she is arrested and sentenced to freeze. But her courage helps to keep her alive until her actions can be proven correct. Fiction.

Ray, N. L. **There Was This Man Running.** Macmillan Publishing Co., 1981. ISBN 0-02-775760-9.

The Macken family gets involved with evil, deception, and a being from another world. But their love for each other helps give them the courage to fight and win against terrible odds. Fiction.

Waldorf, Mary. **Thousand Camps.** Houghton Mifflin Co., 1982. ISBN 0-395-31866-1.

Chloe goes to spend the summer on the California coast to claim her inheritance—Mil Campos Ranch. But she and Joaquin, a local boy, must travel back in time to find a document that will save the ranch from developers. Fiction.

Webster, Joanne. **The Love Genie.** Elsevier/Nelson Books, 1980. ISBN 0-525-66699-0.

Jennie's genie can make her beautiful, do her homework, and help her get the boy she wants. But having a genie isn't as easy as it seems, and soon Jennie has to make a big decision. Fiction.

Westall, Robert. **The Scarecrows.** Greenwillow Books, 1981. ISBN 0-688-00612-4.

Thirteen-year-old Simon cannot cope with his rage toward his mother and his new stepfather. Three scarecrows and an old mill become the focus of his strange hallucinations—which begin to seem like reality to Simon. Is he going crazy? Fiction.

Willett, John. **The Singer in the Stone.** Houghton Mifflin Co., 1981. ISBN 0-395-30374-5.

Rubythroat, a Lost One who sings and dreams, enters the life and heart of Angelina of the Plain People. From Rubythroat, Angelina learns to imagine, question, and dream—all acts that her people discourage. Fiction.

Wiseman, David. **Jeremy Visick.** Houghton Mifflin Co., 1981. ISBN 0-395-30449-0.

Matthew is drawn almost against his will to a tombstone that marks the grave of three men who died in a mine accident a hundred years ago. The fourth victim, twelve-year-old Jeremy, was never found. Then one day Jeremy's spirit takes Matthew down into Wheal Maid. There Matthew risks his own life to give peace to Jeremy. Fiction.

Yep, Laurence. **Dragon of the Lost Sea.** Harper & Row, Publishers, 1982. ISBN 0-06-026746-1.

Shimmer is a proud young dragon, and Thorn is a scrawny orphan boy. They make an unlikely team as they fight Civet, a witch who has stolen the sea, which was Shimmer's home. As the dragon and the boy become involved in fantastic battles, they come to respect and love each other. Fiction.

FOLKLORE

Curtis, Edward S., compiler (editor John Bierhorst). **The Girl Who Married a Ghost and Other Tales from the North American Indian.** Photographs by author. Four Winds Press, 1980. ISBN 0-590-07505-5.

Stories of the supernatural, stories of daily life—here are nine American Indian tales from the Northwest, California, the Plains, Alaska, the North Woods, and the Southwest. The stories are illustrated by beautiful photographs. Fiction.

Diamond, Donna. **Swan Lake.** Illus. by author. Holiday House, 1980. ISBN 0-8234-0356-4.

Prince Siegfried's love for the swan queen Odette is frustrated by an evil sorcerer in this fairy-tale version of the famous ballet. Fiction.

HISTORY: FACT AND FICTION

Aaron, Chester. **Gideon.** J. B. Lippincott Co., 1982. ISBN 0-397-31992-4.

Gideon is twelve when the Nazis move into Poland in 1939 and begin their brutal campaign against the Jews. His non-Jewish appearance and remarkable daring, skill, and luck see him through the Warsaw ghetto uprising and the horrors of a concentration camp. Fiction.

Baldwin, Margaret. **The Boys Who Saved the Children.** Jem Books, 1981. ISBN 0-671-43603-1.

This is the story of how some courageous boys tried to save the children of Lodz, Poland, from dying in a Nazi concentration camp during World War II. Adapted from *Growing Up in the Holocaust* by Ben Edelbaum. Nonfiction.

Clapp, Patricia. **Witches' Children: A Story of Salem.** Lothrop, Lee & Shepard Books, 1982. ISBN 0-688-00890-9.

Thirteen-year-old Mary Warren tells how she and a group of young girls in seventeenth-century Massachusetts begin to have fits of screaming, convulsions, and strange visions. The hysterical reaction of the townspeople to all this leads to the famous and tragic Salem Witch Trials. Fiction.

Collier, James Lincoln, and Christopher Collier. **Jump Ship to Freedom.** Delacorte Press, 1981. ISBN 0-440-04205-4.

Daniel, a fourteen-year-old slave, escapes from his dishonest master in 1787. He needs to cash some pay notes his father earned as a soldier during the American Revolution. Daniel wants the money to purchase his family's freedom. Fiction.

Degens, T. **The Visit.** Viking Press, 1982. ISBN 0-670-74712-2.

Kate Hoffman has always looked forward to seeing her fun-loving Aunt Sylvia. Then she discovers the diary of Aunt Kate, Sylvia's sister who died mysteriously in World War II. The diary details the sisters' experiences in the Hitler Youth movement and shockingly reveals Sylvia's involvement in her sister's death. Fiction.

Dyer, T. A. **A Way of His Own.** Houghton Mifflin Co., 1981. ISBN 0-395-30443-1.

Crippled Shutok is left by his primitive tribe to die alone on the plains. But with the help of a slave girl, Shutok survives a bitter winter and learns to live without fear and superstition for the first time in his life. Fiction.

Fisher, Leonard Everett. **The Unions.** Illus. by author. Holiday House, 1982. ISBN 0-8234-0434-X.

This is the story of the American labor movement from the seventeenth through the nineteenth century. The development of industry, poor working conditions, and the desire of workers to live decently all contributed to the growth of unions. Nonfiction.

Fleischman, Paul. **Path of the Pale Horse.** Harper & Row, Publishers, 1983. ISBN 0-06-021904-1.

Asclepius "Lep" Nye, a doctor's apprentice, has his faith in medical science shaken during the Philadelphia yellow-fever epidemic in 1793. The quackery and double-dealing he sees leave him painfully aware of his own limitations and those of medical science. Fiction.

García, Ann O'Neal. **Spirit on the Wall.** Holiday House, 1982. ISBN 0-8234-0447-1.

Mat-Maw defies the customs of her clan of Stone Age cave dwellers by preventing her daughter from killing her crippled baby. The baby, Em, grows into a beautiful young girl with a marvelous artistic gift. Fiction.

Hurmence, Belinda. **A Girl Called Boy.** Clarion Books, 1982. ISBN 0-395-31022-9.

Eleven-year-old Blanche Overtha Yancey ("Boy" for short) doesn't share her father's pride in their black ancestors. Then she is magically transported back to the 1850s. She quickly learns some painful truths about slavery—and about herself. Fiction.

Marzollo, Jean. **Halfway Down Paddy Lane.** Dial Press, 1981. ISBN 0-8037-3329-1.

Fifteen-year-old Kate Calambra is transported back in time to 1850. She is thought to be Kate O'Hara, a member of an Irish immigrant family. To survive, she must play that role and remain undetected. As Kate O'Hara, she soon learns about the brutal conditions in a New England textile factory and the often violent bigotry against the Irish. Kate also must cope with her strong attraction to Patrick, who thinks he is her brother. Fiction.

Moeri, Louise. **Save Queen of Sheba.** E. P. Dutton, 1981. ISBN 0-525-33202-2. Flare Books, 1982 (paperback). ISBN 0-380-58529-4.

Twelve-year old King David and his sister, Queen of Sheba, are traveling to Oregon when their wagon train is wiped out by Sioux Indians. The children must survive and try to find their parents. Fiction.

O'Dell, Scott. **Sarah Bishop.** Houghton Mifflin Co., 1980. ISBN 0-395-29185-2.

The Revolutionary War quickly brings danger and tragedy to Sarah Bishop. Her brother dies soon after joining the American army, and her father dies when he is tarred and feathered by the British Patriots. Now a fugitive, Sarah flees to the wilderness, where she struggles to build a new life of her own. Fiction.

Payne, Elizabeth. **The Pharaohs of Ancient Egypt.** Landmark Books, 1981. ISBN 0-384-84699-0.

Learn the story behind the mummies and pyramids. This book uses the work of archaeologists to recreate the civilization of ancient Egypt, a civilization that lasted over three thousand years. Nonfiction.

Skurzynski, Gloria. **Manwolf.** Clarion Books, 1981. ISBN 0-395-30079-7.

Adam, a boy in fourteenth-century Poland, has a disease that causes him to look like a werewolf. His mother, Danusha, tries to shield him from the world, but Adam's deformities are eventually exposed. From that moment, he must suffer because of everyone's ignorance and superstition. Fiction.

Wiseman, David. **Thimbles.** Houghton Mifflin Co., 1982. ISBN 0-395-31867-X.

Catherine Aiken is sent to stay with her grandmother because of the troubles caused by her father's union activities. At her grandmother's house she discovers two mysterious thimbles that transport her back to 1819. There she becomes involved in civil rights demonstrations and in the lives of two girls from different social classes. Fiction.

Wisler, G. Clifton. **Winter of the Wolf.** Elsevier/Nelson Books, 1981. ISBN 0-525-66716-4.

Fourteen-year-old T.J. is left in charge of the family's Texas homestead during the Civil War. One day T.J. saves the life of a Comanche youth during an Indian raid. Despite the suspicion and hostility of friends and family, the two become close friends. Together they battle an enormous wolf that the Comanches believe is the devil. Fiction.

HUMOR

Brandreth, Gyles. **Biggest Tongue Twister Book in the World.** Rev. ed. Illus. Alex Chin. Sterling Publishing Co., 1980. ISBN 0-8069-4594-X.

Readers who can say "I go by Blue Goose bus" quickly, three times, without making a mistake will not need this book. The rest of you need to practice your tongue twisting. You will find several hundred challenging examples here. Nonfiction.

Branscum, Robbie. **The Murder of Hound Dog Bates.** Viking Press, 1982. ISBN 0-670-49521-2.

Certain that one of the three aunts he lives with has poisoned his dog, Sass turns detective. He enlists the aid of Kelly O'Kelly, a good-natured stranger who has come to rural Arkansas searching for "a good-cookin' wife." Fiction.

Butterworth, William E. **Moose, the Thing, and Me.** Houghton Mifflin Co., 1982. ISBN 0-395-32077-1.

When Moose Hanrahan, a six-foot-five, 250-pound freshman, comes to Ludwell School, he refuses to play football. He would rather race go-carts. Fellow student "inmates" Runt Peters and Number Three devise a comic plan to get Moose on the field—and save their own skins. Fiction.

Corbett, Scott. **Jokes to Read in the Dark.** Illus. Annie Gusman. Unicorn Books, 1980. ISBN 0-525-32796-7 (ISBN 0-525-45052-1, paperback).

The author warns you never to read more than ten pages of bad jokes at one sitting. These groaners—limericks, knock-knock jokes, puns, epitaphs, and elephant stories—will give you something to do for a few hours. But remember, no more than ten pages at a time! Nonfiction.

Deary, Terry. **Calamity Kate.** Illus. Charlotte Firmin. Carolrhoda Books, 1982. ISBN 0-87614-195-5.

The Warmer Sisters insure Calamity Kate's life for a million dollars when she stars in a silent movie, *The Dangers of Daphne,* for their studio. So who put a real crocodile in the water with Calamity? Who meddled with the train's brakes and the buzz saw? Director Otto Premiere? Co-star Hunk Marvel? Fiction.

Deary, Terry. **The Custard Kid.** Illus. Charlotte Firmin. Carolrhoda Books, 1982. ISBN 0-87614-188-2.

Charged with kidnapping Calamity Kate in Deadwood, the Custard Kid may not make it to Hollywood, where he wants to be a stunt man in silent films. Fiction.

Gilson, Jamie. **Can't Catch Me, I'm the Gingerbread Man.** Lothrop, Lee & Shepard books, 1981. ISBN 0-688-00435-0 (ISBN 0-688-00436-9, library binding).

Twelve-year-old Mitch becomes the only male finalist in the

national ABC Bakeathon. Then his parents' natural-food store is destroyed by fire. So Mitch travels to the finals in Miami Beach, hoping that his gingerbread recipe will win the $30,000 first prize and save his family. Fiction.

Gilson, Jamie. **Dial Leroi Rupert, DJ.** Illus. John Wallner. Lothrop, Lee & Shepard Books, 1979. ISBN 0-688-41888-0 (ISBN 0-688-51888-5, library binding).

Mitch, Lenny, and Aaron have to pay for an expensive flower pot they broke accidentally. So they form a jazz combo and perform on Chicago trains. When they seek help from DJ Leroi Rupert, they soon become the Backward Screams, concert stars. Fiction.

Manes, Stephen. **Be a Perfect Person in Just Three Days!** Illus. Tom Huffman. Clarion Books, 1982. ISBN 0-89919-064-2.

A book falls off a library shelf and hits Milo Crinkley on the head. The book is *Be a Perfect Person in Just Three Days!* by Dr. K. Pinkerton Silverfish. Dr. Silverfish's book promises to change Milo's imperfect life. But Milo wonders how three days can change the effects of many years. Fiction.

McMillan, Bruce, and Brett McMillan. **Puniddles.** Photographs by Bruce McMillan. Houghton Mifflin Co., 1982. ISBN 0-395-32082-8.

Are you good at figuring out puns and riddles? How about puniddles? Puniddles are punny riddles whose only clues are pairs of photographs. See how many you can solve! Nonfiction.

Park, Barbara. **Skinnybones.** Alfred A. Knopf, 1982. ISBN 0-394-94988-9.

Thirteen-year-old Alex Frankovitch is a "real stinky" baseball player, but he loves to make people laugh. When T.J. Stoner, baseball superstar and champion braggart, makes life miserable for Alex, he fights back with his only weapon: "Booga Booga!" Fiction.

Peck, Robert Newton. **Basket Case.** Doubleday & Co., 1979. ISBN 0-385-14362-3.

When seven-foot-tall Courtney Dribble transfers to Graffiti Prep School, everyone hopes he will bring the basketball team out of the league's cellar. But Courtney plays well only when he hears schnitzelboop music! So Graffiti's ace prankster, Higbee Hartburn, sets out to find a schnitzelboop and someone to play it. Fiction.

Pinkwater, Daniel. **The Snarkout Boys and the Avocado of Death.** Lothrop, Lee & Shepard Books, 1982. ISBN 0-688-00871-2.

Walter, Winston, and Rat "snark out" all the time. When Rat's uncle disappears, their snarkouts get crazier and crazier. Will they be able to save the world from the space-realtors? Will Walter ever learn to like avocados? Fiction.

Pinkwater, Daniel M. **Yobgorgle: Mystery Monster of Lake Ontario.** Clarion Books, 1979. ISBN 0-395-28970-X.

Eugene Winklemen is spending two weeks with his uncle in Rochester, New York. While there, Eugene joins eccentric Professor Ambrose McFwain in pursuit of Yobgorgle, a mysterious sea monster said to live in nearby Lake Ontario. Fiction.

Pownall, David. **The Bunch from Bananas.** Illus. Frank Fitzgerald. Macmillan Publishing Co., 1981. ISBN 0-02-775090-6.

When Bernard catches Diablo Dick singlehandedly, he becomes a celebrated crimebuster in Santa Margarita del Banana. Soon his father, Big Fat Joe, who is a retired detective, and Dormitory McBride, the town's sleepy sheriff, must help Bernard crack eight other crime cases that pop up in Santa Margarita. Fiction.

Rosenbloom, Joseph. **Doctor Knock-Knock's Official Knock-Knock Dictionary.** Illus. Joyce Behr. Sterling Publishing Co., 1979. ISBN 0-8069-4536-2.

"Knock-knock." "Who's there?" You will grin and groan when Jaguar, Fiddlesticks, Tarzan, Toyota, and several hundred others come knock-knocking—all in alphabetical order. Fiction.

Rounds, Glen. **Mr. Yowder, the Peripatetic Sign Painter.** Illus. by author. Holiday House, 1980. ISBN 0-8234-0370-X.

In one of these three tall tales, traveling sign-painter Xenon Zebulon Yowder trades a sign for a feeble lion. Then he puts the lion's roar into capsules to sell to circuses. In the other two stories, Xenon wins control of a steamboat in a card game and helps direct a body-building course for a bull snake. Later Yowder rides the snake when he hunts buffalo for the army. Fiction.

Schulz, Charles M. **Dr. Beagle and Mr. Hyde.** Illus. by author. Holt, Rinehart & Winston, 1981. ISBN 0-03-059862-1.

Good grief! Peppermint Patty goes out with Pig-Pen while Snoopy takes Woodstock's friends camping in this collection of "Peanuts" comic strips. Fiction.

Schulz, Charles M. **Things I Learned After It Was Too Late (And Other Minor Truths).** Holt, Rinehart & Winston, 1981. ISBN 0-03-059264-X.

Have you noticed that classes can ruin your grade average? Or that being crabby all day makes you hungry? Charlie Brown, Snoopy, and the other "Peanuts" characters offer comments like these about life that should make everyone happier and wiser. Fiction.

Stine, Jovial Bob, and Jane Stine. **The Sick of Being Sick Book.** Illus. Carol Nicklaus. E. P. Dutton, 1980. ISBN 0-525-39290-4.

Take the "ick" out of being sick! Here are ways to get sympathy when you are ill, recipes to beat the bed-tray blahs, and advice on how to survive daytime TV. There is also a painless quiz to determine what kind of patient you are. Some sick jokes are included (of course). Fiction.

LOVE AND FRIENDSHIP

Asher, Sandy. **Summer Begins.** Elsevier/Nelson, 1980. ISBN 0-525-66696-6.

Thirteen-year-old Summer Smith writes an editorial for her school newspaper speaking out against a Christmas pageant in which students of all religions must participate. The editorial causes trouble, but Summer also gets noticed by handsome Rod Whitman. Fiction.

Bates, Betty. **Love Is like Peanuts.** Holiday House, 1980. ISBN 0-8234-0402-1. Archway Paperbacks, 1981 (paperback). ISBN 0-671-56109-X.

Fourteen-year-old Marianne Mandic has a job babysitting Catsy Kranz, a child with brain damage. Soon Marianne finds herself falling in love with Toby, Catsy's older brother. During their summer together, Toby teaches Marianne that there is much more to a relationship than physical attraction. Fiction.

Beckman, Delores. **My Own Private Sky.** E. P. Dutton, 1980. ISBN 0-525-35510-3.

Eleven-year-old Arthur Elliott's first summer in California is memorable because of his new sitter, Mrs. Jenny Kearns. She is an unusual sixty-year-old woman who teaches Arthur to face his fears. Arthur is soon tested when Jenny loses a leg in a tragic accident. Fiction.

Bolton, Carole. **The Good-Bye Year.** Lodestar Books, 1982. ISBN 0-525-66787-3.

Life in 1939 is not simple for thirteen-year-old Rosemary Beedy. She dreams of being a glamorous movie star. But Rosemary is also caught up in a new romance. And to add to her emotional confusion, Rosemary learns she must move away from the hometown she loves. Fiction.

Borisoff, Norman. **Bewitched and Bewildered: A Spooky Love Story.** Photographs by Harold Roth. Laurel-Leaf Books, 1982. ISBN 0-440-90905-8.

Michael loves Nicole, but there is something strange about her. How else could he explain the fact he can still see her—and talk to her—after she has left on a vacation? Fiction.

Carrick, Carol. **Some Friend!** Illus. Donald Carrick. Clarion Books, 1979. ISBN 0-395-28966-1.

Mike has always let Rob be the boss in their friendship, but one day Rob pushes too far. Mike struggles with his emotions when he realizes that he has to confront Rob or lose their friendship. Fiction.

Conford, Ellen. **Anything for a Friend.** Archway Paperbacks, 1981. ISBN 0-671-56069-7.

Eleven-year-old Wallis Greene has lived in six different cities. Each move is exciting, but it is hard to find new friends. Her latest move to New York, however, teaches Wallis some valuable lessons about making friends and about being a good friend herself. Fiction.

Conford, Ellen. **Hail, Hail Camp Timberwood.** Illus. Gail Owens. Archway Paperbacks, 1980. ISBN 0-671-42685-0.

Melanie Kessler's first summer at camp becomes unforgettable when she meets a very special boy named Steve. But Melanie's growing relationship with Steve is threatened when her bunkmate begins bullying her. With the help and advice of Steve's younger brother, Doug, Melanie is able to confront her bunkmate. Fiction.

Cuyler, Margery. **The Trouble with Soap.** Unicorn Books, 1982. ISBN 0-525-45111-0.

Laurie's best friend, Soap, causes her to get suspended from public school. So Laurie persuades her parents to let her go to a local private school. Soap is at this school, and soon Laurie discovers she must make painful choices between Soap and the chance to make new friends. Fiction.

Eyerly, Jeannette. **If I Loved You Wednesday.** Archway Paperbacks, 1982. ISBN 0-671-43491-8.

Dennis Trimble is overweight and clumsy. Then he falls in love with Ms. Carr, his new English teacher. Dennis decides to lose weight and get a job so he can proclaim his love to Ms. Carr. But then disaster strikes. Ms. Carr becomes divorced and leaves town. Will Dennis ever be able to recover from his love for her? Fiction.

Fox, Paula. **A Place Apart.** Signet Vista Books, 1982. ISBN 0-451-11283-0.

When she loses her father, thirteen-year-old Victoria Finch has to face many sudden changes in her life. Her move to a small town is difficult until she meets Hugh Todd. With Hugh, Victoria begins a friendship that no one else can understand. But it is a friendship that changes forever the way Victoria looks at herself. Fiction.

Gauch, Patricia Lee. **Fridays.** G. P. Putnam's Sons, 1979. ISBN 0-399-20703-1.

Corey Martin's eighth-grade year becomes even more confusing when she becomes a member of a special group. Corey begins to feel there is something wrong with the group. But not until the members turn on one of their own does Corey fully realize the group's power to hurt. Fiction.

Grohskopf, Bernice. **End of Summer.** Flare Books, 1982. ISBN 0-380-79293-1.

During a summer in Maine, Maggie Widgerley meets Tony Wilson, a handsome young Englishman. Maggie is soon deeply in love with Tony. However, when Tony insists on visiting her in her hometown, his irresistible charm comes between Maggie and her best friend. The events that follow threaten to destroy Maggie's romance and hurt her friendship. Fiction.

Hart, Bruce, and Carole Hart. **Waiting Games.** Flare Books, 1981. ISBN
0-380-79012-2.

Jessie decides to let her love for Michael develop into a sexual
relationship. But after they spend a summer apart, Jessie decides
to rethink her relationship with Michael. Should she break off
with Michael permanently? Mature situations. Fiction.

Hest, Amy. **Maybe Next Year. . . .** Clarion Books, 1982. ISBN 0-89919-
063-4.

Twelve-year-old Kate Newman's love of ballet begins to cause
problems for her when it takes valuable time away from her
guardian grandmother. Kate must now decide whether she can
really afford to make ballet a career if it takes her away from
people who love and need her. Fiction.

Howe, Fanny. **Yeah, But.** Flare Books, 1982. ISBN 0-380-79186-2.

Fourteen-year-old Casey Quick is moving to a wealthy part of
town with her aunt and uncle. But because of this move, Casey
discovers she must make difficult decisions about her boyfriend,
Willie, and her new friend, Treat. Fiction.

Johnston, Norma. **The Sanctuary Tree.** Tempo Books, 1982. ISBN 0-
448-17005-1.

The many changes taking place in her life in 1900 make Tish
Sterling feel much older than her fifteen years. When her boyfriend Kenneth moves away, both Tish's performance in school
and her relationships with her friends suffer. It takes a family
crisis for Tish to recognize the good things in her life and accept
the uncertainties of her future. Fiction.

Knudsen, James. **Just Friends.** Flare Books, 1982. ISBN 0-380-80481-6.

Blake Webb's friendship with Libby Esterly and Spencer Fredrick
makes his junior year of high school great. Then he notices that
Libby and Spencer are beginning to leave him out of their activities. Though he is hurt and confused, Blake tries to understand
his part in these changing relationships. Fiction.

Lyle, Katie Letcher. **Dark but Full of Diamonds.** Coward, McCann &
Geoghegan, 1981. ISBN 0-698-20517-0.

When he was twelve, Scott Dabney had a crush on his swimming
coach, Hilah Brown. Now that she has returned after four years,
his feelings for her deepen. But Hilah begins dating Scott's father,

and they eventually announce their plans to marry. Scott does not think he will ever be able to overcome his anger and accept Hilah as his stepmother. Fiction.

Pascal, Francine. **Hangin' Out with Cici.** Archway Paperbacks, 1978. ISBN 0-671-43879-4.

Thirteen-year-old Victoria Martin is nearly expelled from school. Then she gets caught smoking marijuana at a party. But Victoria has even stranger experiences when she is transported back to the 1940s and meets her mother, Cici, as a teenager. This bizarre event drastically changes Victoria's understanding of herself and of her relationship with her mother. Fiction.

Peck, Richard. **Father Figure.** Signet Vista Books, 1979. ISBN 0-451-08846-8.

When seventeen-year-old Jim Atwater loses his mother, Jim and his brother have to face a summer visit with a stranger—their own father. His brother has always looked up to Jim for advice and help. Now Jim is afraid he will lose his little brother to a father he cannot yet accept. Fiction.

Peck, Robert Newton. **Banjo.** Illus. Andrew Glass. Alfred A. Knopf, 1982. ISBN 0-394-85934-6 (ISBN 0-394-95394-0, library binding).

When Alvin Dickinson picks Banjo Byler as his essay partner, he never imagines that Banjo's subject will be a man they fear, Jake Horse, an old hermit. Finding Jake leads Alvin and Banjo into danger, but Jake himself is not as frightening as they had imagined. Fiction.

Pfeffer, Susan Beth. **Starring Peter and Leigh.** Laurel-Leaf Books, 1980. ISBN 0-440-98200-6.

All sixteen-year-old Leigh Thorpe wants is to give up her lifetime of acting and be an average teenager. With the help of her step-brother, Peter, Leigh learns to live a normal life. Then a special job offer forces Leigh to reconsider her feelings about acting and her relationship with Peter. Fiction.

Robinson, Barbara. **Temporary Times, Temporary Places.** Harper & Row, Publishers, 1982. ISBN 0-06-025039-9.

In her fifteenth summer, Janet experiences the joy and pain of falling in love for the first time. Janet soon has a chance to compare her experiences to those of her Aunt May. Aunt May is visiting Janet's family in order to get over her latest love affair.

From talking to Aunt May, Janet realizes that people cannot always withdraw from life for fear of being hurt by others. Fiction.

Roe, Kathy Gibson. **Goodbye, Secret Place.** Houghton Mifflin Co., 1982. ISBN 0-395-31864-5.

Whitney Bennett has a twisted idea about the meaning of friendship. These thoughts almost destroy the special relationship she has with her friend Robin. Then, when Robin's family move away, Whitney is faced with a terrible feeling of loss she is not sure she can handle. Fiction.

Sachs, Marilyn. **Bus Ride.** Illus. Amy Rowen. E. P. Dutton, 1980. ISBN 0-525-27325-5 (ISBN 0-525-45048-3, paperback).

On the daily bus rides home from school, a friendship develops between Judy and Ernie. They listen to each others' problems and offer advice about their relationships with other people. But when Ernie discovers that Judy has not been totally honest with him, they have a tense confrontation that makes both of them rethink their friendship. Fiction.

Sachs, Marilyn. **Class Pictures.** E. P. Dutton, 1980. ISBN 0-525-27985-7.

As she looks back through old class pictures, Pat traces her friendship with Lolly from kindergarten through high school graduation. Pat remembers that when they were young she was Lolly's protector. But when Lolly turned into the class beauty their relationship changed—and not always for the better. Fiction.

Sachs, Marilyn. **Hello . . . Wrong Number.** Illus. Pamela Johnson. E. P. Dutton, 1981. ISBN 0-525-31629-9.

When Angie Rogers dials a wrong number in her attempt to phone the best-looking boy in school, she has an interesting conversation with a total stranger. In the weeks following the call, Angie begins to depend on her new "telephone friend," but her desire to meet him face-to-face almost destroys their special relationship. Fiction.

Scoppettone, Sandra. **A Long Time between Kisses.** Harper & Row, Publishers, 1982. ISBN 0-06-025229-4 (ISBN 0-06-025230-8, library binding).

Billie James's sixteenth summer is a memorable one. First, she decides to dye her hair bright purple. Then Billie breaks up with her boyfriend, rescues a senile neighborhood "character" from a diet of dog food, watches her father freak out on angel dust, and falls in love with a young man with multiple sclerosis. Each of these events has a strong impact on Billie's outlook on life. And, surprisingly enough, almost everything makes Billie feel more positive about herself. Fiction.

Snyder, Anne, and Louis Pelletier. **Two Point Zero.** Signet Vista Books, 1982. ISBN 0-686-97214-7.

To pay her college expenses, Kate Fleming works for an illegal tutoring service for athletes. When a campus newspaper writer threatens to expose the service and all who are involved, Kate finds herself making hard decisions that will affect the rest of her life. Fiction.

Stirling, Nora. **You Would If You Loved Me.** Flare Books, 1982. ISBN 0-380-57984-7.

Trudy Munroe is in a dream world when she dates Tom. But he wants more from Trudy than she is willing to give. For Trudy, deciding not to give in to Tom's sexual demands helps her realize what a shallow person he is. But now she must also learn to accept the fact that she was partly to blame by leading Tom on. Mature situations. Fiction.

Strasser, Todd. **Friends till the End.** Delacorte Press, 1981. ISBN 0-440-02750-0.

Senior David Gilbert devotes most of his time to soccer and his girlfriend until Howie Jamison moves to town. David's reluctance to be Howie's friend abruptly changes when Howie develops leukemia. Now David has to face the idea of death coming to someone his own age. From these thoughts, David develops the desire to comfort and help Howie. Fiction.

Sunshine, Tina. **An X-Rated Romance.** Flare Books, 1982. ISBN 0-380-79905-7.

Emily Josephson tries to help her best friend Sara get noticed by her eighth-grade English teacher. The result is a series of hilariously complicated situations that only Sara and Emily can really understand. Fiction.

Van Steenwyk, Elizabeth. **Rivals on Ice.** Illus. Rondi Anderson. Albert Whitman & Co., 1979. ISBN 0-8075-7071-0.

Twelve-year-old Tucker Cameron hoped to win the novice ice-skating championship in her region until talented Sara Mars moves in. Tucker is soon caught between her competitive spirit and her feelings of sympathy for Sara and her personal problems. When she decides to help Sara, Tucker discovers she has created a difficult situation for herself. Fiction.

Webster, Joanne. **Gypsy Gift.** Lodestar Books, 1981. ISBN 0-525-66763-6.

Handsome gypsy Rollo gives Cassie Prior the ability to see into the future. But when Cassie becomes bored with Rollo, he begins to seek revenge against her. Only slowly does Rollo realize how destructive his powers can be. Fiction.

Winthrop, Elizabeth. **Marathon Miranda.** Holiday House, 1979. ISBN 0-8234-0349-1.

Twelve-year-old Miranda Bartlett has always been a physical failure until she meets Phoebe, who introduces her to the pleasures of running. Through her new dedication to running, Miranda finds solutions to many of her problems as she learns to set and reach her own goals. Fiction.

Winthrop, Elizabeth. **Miranda in the Middle.** Holiday House, 1980. ISBN 0-8234-0422-6.

At thirteen, Miranda Bartlett finds herself in the middle of several difficult situations—with her best friend, her brother, a new friend, her future stepgrandmother, and a neighborhood group determined to save an old church. But when Miranda finally learns to face these situations honestly, she discovers her problems seem to resolve themselves. Fiction.

Wood, Phyllis Anderson. **This Time Count Me In.** Westminster Press, 1980. ISBN 0-664-32665-X. Archway Paperbacks, 1981 (paperback). ISBN 0-671-42689-3.

Sophomore Peggy Marklee chooses to transfer from a private to a public school because she wants a chance to meet different kinds of people. Eventually she finds new friends and the boyfriend she always dreamed about. But Peggy also becomes unexpectedly involved in tensions when she sees two boys in her reading class steal a teacher's wallet. Fiction.

Yep, Laurence. **Kind Hearts and Gentle Monsters.** Harper & Row, Publishers, 1982. ISBN 0-06-026732-1.

A chain letter is directly responsible for getting Charley Sabini and Chris Pomeroy together, but only because Charley becomes angry when Chris sends it. An unusual and surprising friendship develops between the two, as both realize they need each other for different reasons. Fiction.

Yolen, Jane. **The Gift of Sarah Barker.** Viking Press, 1981. ISBN 0-670-64580-X.

Fourteen-year-old Sarah Barker had lived by strict Shaker rules since her mother joined the New Vale religious community when Sarah was four. Then Sarah falls in love with Abel Church. Driven out of the Shaker community because of this love, Sarah realizes Abel is now the only person she can turn to. Fiction.

MYSTERY AND CRIME

Adler, C. S. **The Evidence That Wasn't There.** Clarion Books, 1982. ISBN 0-89919-117-7.

Kim, a high school student, just doesn't like Mr. Orlop. She suspects his effort to claim a large inheritance for the Davises is just a con to cheat them out of a lot of money. But she finds herself in great danger when she tries to expose Orlop. Fiction.

Asimov, Isaac. **The Key Word and Other Mysteries.** Illus. Rod Burke. Camelot Books, 1979. ISBN 0-380-43224-2.

Larry, a seventh-grader, is the talented son of a city detective. When certain mystery cases puzzle his father, Larry decides to help by discovering and putting together vital clues. Fiction.

Baird, Thomas. **Finding Fever.** Harper & Row, Publishers, 1982. ISBN 0-06-020353-6 (ISBN 0-06-020354-4, library binding).

When his sister's dog, Fever, is stolen, fifteen-year-old Benny O'Bryan risks danger to find the dog. But there are two immediate problems: Benny does not even like Fever, and he must accept the help of Robert Striller, someone he also dislikes. Fiction.

Bennett, Jay. **The Executioner.** Flare Books, 1982. ISBN 0-380-79160-9.

Bruce Kendall, a high school junior, can't forget the night he, Ed, and Elaine—all drunk—were riding home in Raymond's car. He can't forget that he caused an accident in which Raymond died. Someone else can't forget either. The executioner intends to make Ed, Elaine, and Bruce pay for what they have done. Fiction.

Bethancourt, T. Ernesto. **Doris Fein: Deadly Aphrodite.** Holiday House, 1982. ISBN 0-8234-0445-5.

At seventeen Doris has inherited a newspaper and a fortune. One day she checks into a local health spa to lose some weight. There Doris discovers movie stars, high-society people—and murder. But with the help of Bruno, her houseman, and Larry, her childhood sweetheart, Doris solves a murder mystery. Fiction.

Bethancourt, T. Ernesto. **Doris Fein: Murder Is No Joke.** Holiday House, 1982. ISBN 0-8234-0468-4.

Seventeen-year-old Doris Fein meets tall, handsome comedian Steven Sachs. Soon a romance develops between them. But Steve's comedy act covers terror. A series of violent deaths leads Doris into more danger than she expected. Fiction.

Brow, Thea. **The Secret Cross of Lorraine.** Illus. Allen Say. Parnassus Press, 1981. ISBN 0-395-30344-3.

A high school student and mystery reader, Twyla gets a chance to do some sleuthing in France. She becomes involved with former French Resistance fighters of World War II while trying to locate the owner of a lost Cross of Lorraine. Fiction.

Cavanna, Betty. **Stamp Twice for Murder.** William Morrow & Co., 1981. ISBN 0-688-00700-7.

Sixteen-year-old Jan and her family spend the summer in France in a cottage they have inherited. While there, Jan finds romance and danger as she tries to learn the reason for her great-uncle's murder. Fiction.

Christian, Mary Blount. **The Firebug Mystery.** Illus. Allen Davis. Albert Whitman & Co., 1982. ISBN 0-8075-2444-1.

Brock and Gaby are teenage friends involved in a strange situation: half-finished buildings are being burned to the ground. Could it be the work of a school associate who takes photos of the fires in progress? Or could their own fathers, the owner and contractor of the buildings, be involved? Fiction.

Christian, Mary Blount. **The Mystery of the Double Double Cross.** Illus. Marie DeJohn. Albert Whitman & Co., 1982. ISBN 0-8075-5374-3.

When his brother becomes ill, sixteen-year-old Jeff agrees to take over his chauffering job. During a trip with an important oil executive, Jeff and the man are kidnapped. Now they are being held hostage in a beach house that is directly in the path of a hurricane. Fiction.

Christopher, Matt. **The Return of the Headless Horseman.** Illus. James McLaughlin. Westminster Press, 1982. ISBN 0-664-32690-0.

Fishing late one night, Steve and Jim see a horse and its headless rider. Steve hopes this story will help save his father's newspaper. But then another newspaper prints the story first. Steve and Jim set out to solve the mystery so Steve's father can have an even bigger story. Fiction.

Cohen, Daniel. **Frauds, Hoaxes, and Swindles.** Illus. David Prebenna. Laurel-Leaf Books, 1980. ISBN 0-440-92699-5.

The German shoemaker who dressed in a military uniform and arrested the mayor, the Frenchman who sold the Eiffel Tower twice, and the little-known writer who claimed that billionaire Howard Hughes had told him his life story—all are among the six con artists whose stories are revealed here. Nonfiction.

Cohen, Daniel. **Missing! Stories of Strange Disappearances.** Archway Paperbacks, 1980. ISBN 0-671-56052-2.

The truth is really often stranger than fiction. The stories in this book reveal all that is known about six famous cases of people disappearing. Even after years of detective work, these cases are still not solved. Illustrations. Nonfiction.

Coontz, Otto. **Mystery Madness.** Houghton Mifflin Co., 1982. ISBN 0-395-32079-8.

Twelve-year-old Murray overhears a murder being committed during a phone call. All clues point to Murray's college-age sister as the murderer, so Murray decides to sacrifice sleep, friends, and school to clear his sister. But first, he must hire a real detective to help him. Fiction.

David, Andrew. **Famous Criminal Trials.** Lerner Publications Co., 1979. ISBN 0-8225-1427-3.

Here are the stories of eight famous trials: Sacco and Vanzetti, Leopold and Loeb, Bruno Richard Hauptmann, the Rosenbergs, the Chicago Eight, Sirhan Sirhan, and James Earl Ray. These are trials for murder, kidnapping, conspiracy, treason, and assassination. Read all the evidence and then decide how you would have judged the case. Nonfiction.

Dicks, Terrance. **The Baker Street Irregulars in The Case of the Black-mail Boys.** Elsevier/Nelson Books, 1981. ISBN 0-525-66710-5.

A bank robbery, the strange behavior of some friends, and the antics of some clowning window washers lead Dan Robinson and his Baker Street Irregulars to the leader of a theft and blackmail ring. Fiction.

Dicks, Terrance. **The Baker Street Irregulars in The Case of the Cinema Swindle.** Elsevier/Nelson Books, 1980. ISBN 0-525-66728-8.

An attempt to burn a movie theater. A riot at the children's matinee. A kitchen fire in Dan's home. All these strange events lead the Baker Street Irregulars—Dan, Liz, Mickey, and Jeff—to move against the mysterious firebug who is attempting to grab some valuable property. Fiction.

Dicks, Terrance. **The Baker Street Irregulars in The Case of the Cop Catchers.** Lodestar Books, 1982. ISBN 0-525-66765-2.

Detective-Sergeant "Happy" Day is missing. From information he left behind, it looks as if Happy is involved in bribe taking. The Baker Street Irregulars are sure that their friend has been framed. But to find out for certain, they must solve the four cases Happy was working on. Fiction.

Dicks, Terrance. **The Baker Street Irregulars in The Case of the Crooked Kids.** Elsevier/Nelson Books, 1980. ISBN 0-525-66711-3.

While examining the scenes of various thefts, the Baker Street Irregulars notice that toy trains, soft drinks, potato chips, and candy are being stolen along with more valuable items. Irregulars leader Dan Robinson suspects that kids taught by a professional criminal are committing the crimes, but he needs proof. Fiction.

Dicks, Terrance. **The Baker Street Irregulars in The Case of the Ghost Grabbers.** Elsevier/Nelson Books, 1981. ISBN 0-525-66729-6.

Sir Jasper, an old friend of the Baker Street Irregulars, is visited by the ghost of a notorious ancestor. Frightening experiences and a warning from a psychic investigator convince Sir Jasper to leave his house until Dan and the Irregulars can tie all the facts together. Fiction.

Dicks, Terrance. **The Baker Street Irregulars in The Case of the Missing Masterpiece.** Elsevier/Nelson Books, 1979. ISBN 0-525-66656-7.

The Baker Street Irregulars—a group of teenagers led by Dan

Robinson, an avid Sherlock Holmes fan—set out to trace a stolen painting and save a historical mansion. Their investigation involves them with three desperate men who want to get rid of the kids—perhaps even kill them. Fiction.

D'Ignazio, Fred. **Chip Mitchell: The Case of the Stolen Computer Brains.** Illus. Larry Pearson. Lodestar Books, 1982. ISBN 0-525-66790-3.

Chip Mitchell, a seventh-grade computer whiz, solves ten puzzles involving computers and video games. This book invites you to match your detective skills with Chip's, then check the solutions to the puzzles at the end of the book. Fiction.

Dodson, Susan. **The Creep.** Archway Paperbacks, 1980. ISBN 0-671-56087-5.

Sixteen-year-old Sabrina joins the police force to trap a child molester. She always keeps in touch with her back-up force, but when Sabrina learns the "Creep's" identity she takes a foolish chance. Mature situations. Fiction.

Ellerby, Leona. **King Tut's Game Board.** Illus. Susan Hopp. Lerner Publications Co., 1980. ISBN 0-8225-0765-X.

Sixteen-year-old Justin Sanders and his parents vacation in Egypt. Justin's interest in ancient history leads him and mysterious Nathan Alistant into a strange search. In the Valley of the Kings, they make a startling discovery, and Justin hears an incredible story. Fiction.

Elmore, Patricia. **Susannah and the Blue House Mystery.** Illus. John C. Wallner. E. P. Dutton, 1980. ISBN 0-525-40525-9.

Teenagers Susannah and Lucy work to solve one mystery, which leads them to another. Juliet's grandfather disappears, and the girls' search for him opens up another case. Is there a treasure among the junk he left behind that can bring Juliet the money he has promised her? Fiction.

Giff, Patricia Reilly. **Suspect.** Illus. Stephen Marchesi. E. P. Dutton, 1982. ISBN 0-525-45108-0.

Paul Starr, traveling by bus to New York, has his wallet stolen at a roadside restaurant. But while chasing the thief, he finds the body of a woman. When he finds he is a murder suspect, Paul realizes he must solve the mystery himself. Fiction.

Heide, Florence Parry, and Roxanne Heide. **Black Magic at Brillstone.** Albert Whitman & Co., 1981. ISBN 0-8075-0782-2.

Teenagers Liza Webster and Logan Forrest must protect an elderly neighbor, Miss Violet, from a spiritualist who is trying to cheat her out of her inheritance. Fiction.

Heide, Florence Parry, and Roxanne Heide. **Body in the Brillstone Garage.** Albert Whitman & Co., 1980. ISBN 0-8075-0825-X.

Liza Webster, teenage detective, discovers in the garage a body wearing Mr. Greening's warm-up jacket. But when Liza finds a friend to return to the garage with her, the body is gone. Later she runs into Mr. Greening wearing his jacket. Could he be the killer? Liza feels she must solve the mystery and find the murderer. Fiction.

Heide, Florence Parry, and Roxanne Heide. **Face at the Brillstone Window.** Albert Whitman & Co., 1981. ISBN 0-8075-2216-3.

While working as a reporter for her father, Liza Webster is cautioned by friends and a fellow worker to abandon her attempt to prove Robin Keck's innocence. But, Liza wonders, did he shoot the security guard and steal the money, or was he framed? Her interviews about the case soon lead her into danger and discovery. Fiction.

Heide, Florence Parry, and Roxanne Heide. **Mystery of the Forgotten Island.** Illus. Seymour Fleishman. Albert Whitman & Co., 1980. ISBN 0-8075-5376-X.

Teenagers Jay, Cindy, and Dexter come across a chain of lakes, a secluded house on an island, and an old man who claims to be a prisoner—and it all adds up to mystery and danger. Can the trio save Mr. Whitson and, at the same time, help end threats to the wilderness around them? Fiction.

Hildick, E. W. **The Top-Flight Fully-Automated Junior High School Girl Detective.** Illus. Iris Schweitzer. Archway Paperbacks, 1979. ISBN 0-671-43574-4.

Alison, a junior high student, has two goals—to see herself in a TV detective series and to solve a real mystery herself. Now her second dream may come true. She, her younger sister Jeannie, and their friend Emmaline must quickly locate the person who found Emmaline's father's Newcharge credit card and who is buying hundreds of dollars worth of merchandise with it. Fiction.

Hooker, Ruth, and Carole Smith. **The Kidnapping of Anna.** Illus. George Armstrong. Albert Whitman & Co., 1981. ISBN 0-8075-4176-1.

It was supposed to be a quiet Christmas for the Hendersons at the mountain home of some friends. But then the housekeeper is kidnapped. Teenagers Grant and Patti Henderson decide to rescue the housekeeper and clear up a few other mysterious events connected with the house and the surrounding area. Fiction.

Leonard, Constance. **The Marina Mystery.** Dodd, Mead & Co., 1981. ISBN 0-396-07930-X.

After finishing college, Tracy James sails to a Florida marina to find Pete Sturtevant. But instead of romance, she finds murder and a mysterious and sinister yacht. Before the summer is over, Tracy finds many chances to test Pete's advice: "Don't panic. If you stop and think, there's always a way." Fiction.

Macdonald, Shelagh. **Five from Me, Five from You.** André Deutsch, 1981. ISBN 0-233-96554-8.

Pethi and Tini, teenagers on the Greek island Serifos, face excitement and danger as they search for a treasure involving the goddess Athene. Can they escape mysterious strangers? Fiction.

Madison, Arnold. **Great Unsolved Cases.** Illus. Michael Deas. Laurel-Leaf Books, 1980. ISBN 0-440-93099-5.

Match your detective skills with the experts as you read clues about three famous cases—Jack the Ripper, the kidnapping of Charles Lindbergh's son, and Flight 967. Nonfiction.

Milton, Hilary. **Shutterbugs and Car Thieves.** Julian Messner, 1981. ISBN 0-671-44326-7.

Scott, Jimbo, and Ellie stumble upon the headquarters for a stolen-car ring. While trying to get a closer look, Jimbo is grabbed by two men and is put on a truck to be driven to an unknown destination. Scott and Ellie climb aboard and think up a plan to rescue Jimbo and to escape from the dangerous criminals. Fiction.

Murphy, Jim. **Death Run.** Clarion Books, 1982. ISBN 0-89919-065-0.

Four senior high boys accidentally cause another student's death. Detective Wheeler is suspicious and determined to catch them. But Brian, one of the hunted group, thinks he can outwit Wheeler. He has a big problem though—how can he live with his guilt over the death? Fiction.

Nixon, Joan Lowery. **The Kidnapping of Christina Lattimore.** Harcourt Brace Jovanovich, 1979. ISBN 0-15-242657-4.

Although seventeen-year-old Christina Lattimore is from one of the wealthiest families in Houston, she is unhappy with her life. For one thing, her parents seem to have a hard time accepting her for what she is. After she is kidnapped and then released, Christina finds that her family has even less confidence in her than she ever realized. They actually suspect she helped arrange her own kidnapping! Christina wonders how she can prove her innocence. Fiction.

Powers, Bill. **The Weekend.** Photographs by Meryl Joseph. Laurel-Leaf Books, 1979. ISBN 0-440-99063-7.

Fifteen-year-old Jimmy Scott is mistakenly accused of beating an elderly woman. Because of this, he is sentenced to a juvenile detention center. There Jimmy must face a dark world of violence and terror. Fiction.

Rabe, Berniece. **Who's Afraid?** Illus. Maribeth Olson. E. P. Dutton, 1980. ISBN 0-525-42708-2.

Sixteen-year-old Billie Jo leaves an unpleasant family situation to live with her sister's family. On the bus she meets a new friend who gives her a metal box. The box looks harmless enough, but it soon puts Billie Jo, her new family, and new friends in great danger. Fiction.

Roy, Ron. **I Am a Thief.** Illus. Mel Williges. Unicorn Books, 1982. ISBN 0-525-45114-5.

Brad, an eighth-grader, feels lonely. He is new in town, his mother is in school and works at night, and he doesn't mix well with others. Walking in a mall one day, he meets Chet, who involves him in a shoplifting ring. Soon Brad faces danger from both the police and the members of the ring. Fiction.

Shanks, Ann Zane. **Busted Lives: Dialogues with Kids in Jail.** Photographs by author. Delacorte Press, 1982. ISBN 0-440-00839-5.

Recorded talks with teenagers in jail give a realistic and disturbing look at teenage crime and correctional institutions. Further insights are provided by conversations with experts on the causes of delinquency. Nonfiction.

Smaridge, Norah. **The Mysteries in the Commune.** Illus. Robert Handville. Dodd, Mead & Co., 1982. ISBN 0-396-08076-6.

Sixteen-year-old Robin and her friend Jerry have a double mystery to solve when a nearby house becomes a commune. They try to find Emmy's real mother while searching for Adam's true identity and his reason for running away. Fiction.

Smaridge, Norah. **The Mystery in the Old Mansions.** Illus. Robert Handville. Dodd, Mead & Co., 1981. ISBN 0-396-07980-6.

Robin, a fifteen-year-old sleuth, finds two mysteries to solve when she takes a summer job as a guide in an historic house. First the formula for a rare pottery glaze is lost, then Lucinda, another guide, disappears. Fiction.

Snyder, Zilpha Keatley. **The Famous Stanley Kidnapping Case.** Aladdin Books, 1979. ISBN 0-689-70754-1.

Five children, ages five to thirteen, are excited about spending a year in Italy. But their many plans certainly do not include being kidnapped. The experience proves strange and exciting not only for the children, but for their kidnappers also. Fiction.

Sobol, Donald J. **Encyclopedia Brown's Book of Wacky Crimes.** Illus. Ted Enik. Lodestar Books, 1982. ISBN 0-525-66786-5.

Encyclopedia Brown, a ten-year-old detective, sets aside his latest case to share some strange and funny crime stories with his friends. Fiction.

Stegeman, Janet Allais. **Last Seen on Hopper's Lane.** Dial Press, 1982. ISBN 0-8037-4970-8.

A high school girl is taken captive by two drug dealers as she explores a deserted mansion. She faces danger when the older man decides to kill her and his companion. As they try to escape, the two teenagers come to know and trust each other. Fiction.

Yep, Laurence. **The Mark Twain Murders.** Four Winds Press, 1982. ISBN 0-590-07824-0.

There is murder, mystery, and even comedy in this story of Mark Twain and a Confederate plot to defeat the Union during the Civil War. Twain and a fifteen-year-old friend called the Duke of Baywater decide they will risk danger and death in order to expose the plot. Fiction.

POETRY

Larrick, Nancy, editor. **Bring Me All of Your Dreams.** Photographs by Larry Mulvehill. M. Evans & Co., 1980. ISBN 0-87131-313-8.

Do you like to daydream? What kind of dreams do you have when you sleep? This collection of poems is certain to remind you of some of your own experiences with dreams, and even nightmares. Black-and-white photographs are added to try to capture the dream world.

Wallenstein, Barry. **Roller Coaster Kid and Other Poems.** Thomas Y. Crowell Co., 1982. ISBN 0-690-04067-9.

This slim book of poems covers such different subjects as roller coasters, spiders, and love. The poems invite you to compare the ideas in them with your own thoughts. At the end of the book, the poet lets you know what he thinks about each of his poems.

PROBLEMS

Adler, C. S. **The Cat That Was Left Behind.** Clarion Books, 1981. ISBN 0-395-31020-2.

Thirteen-year-old Chad spends the summer on Cape Cod with his new foster family, the Sorenics. But Chad does not want to be part of the family. He is waiting for the day his mother will come back to get him. However, waiting can be lonely, so Chad befriends a stray cat whose trust he has to earn slowly. Fiction.

Armstrong, Louise. **Saving the Big-Deal Baby.** Illus. Jack Hearne. E. P. Dutton, 1980. ISBN 0-525-38805-2 (ISBN 0-525-45050-5, paperback).

How could a baby be a threat to a marriage? Janine and Robbie could only see happiness when they first had P.J. But now the pressures of taking care of a fourteen-month-old are causing the young couple to split apart. Robbie is finding it hard to work, and Janine even has thoughts of physically abusing the baby. They decide to seek help from a group of young couples with similar problems. Fiction.

Avi. **A Place Called Ugly.** Pantheon Books, 1981. ISBN 0-394-84755-5 (ISBN 0-394-94755-X, library binding).

The cottage where fourteen-year-old Owen and his family have spent ten happy summer vacations is going to be bulldozed to make way for a resort hotel. Since the place has many good memories for his family, Owen decides he will fight to save it. The struggle to save the family cottage helps Owen take a step to maturity. Fiction.

Bargar, Gary W. **What Happened to Mr. Forster?** Clarion Books, 1981. ISBN 0-395-31021-0.

During the 1950s, eleven-year-old Louis, the class outsider, gains confidence in himself and his writing from his teacher, Mr. Forster. When parents accuse the teacher of homosexuality, Louis is upset and disturbed. Will his friendship with Mr. Forster have to end now? Mature situations. Fiction.

Bartholomew, Barbara. **Anne and Jay.** Signet Vista Books, 1982. ISBN 0-451-11655-0.

Fifteen-year-old Anne Hollis hates being the "baby" of the family. But when she tries to discover her own identity, she gets involved with a boy who could prove a threat to her father's job and her family's security. Caught in the middle, Anne struggles to discover the truth about Jay and about her own personality. Fiction.

Bates, Betty. **Bugs in Your Ears.** Archway Paperbacks, 1979. ISBN 0-671-41672-3.

Carrie feels completely left out when her mother remarries. Now she has to learn to live with a new stepfather, who has three kids of his own. Will Carrie ever get along with her new family? Fiction.

Bates, Betty. **My Mom, the Money Nut.** Holiday House, 1979. ISBN 0-8234-0347-5. Archway Paperbacks, 1981 (paperback). ISBN 0-671-56065-4.

Fritzi Zimmer wonders why her mother is more interested in material possessions than in her. To try and get her mother's attention, Fritzi works to become a soloist in the school chorus. But even this does not seem to help. Then Fritzi learns some surprising facts about her mother when she visits her grandfather. Fiction.

Bauer, Marion Dane. **Tangled Butterfly.** Clarion Books, 1980. ISBN 0-395-29110-0.

Seventeen-year-old Michelle has withdrawn from the world in a psychotic state. When a young Native American writer tries to help her, she almost destroys his life and his family's happiness.

How can her friends keep trying to save Michelle from herself if she continues to strike out at them? Fiction.

Betancourt, Jeanne. **Smile! How to Cope with Braces.** Illus. Mimi Harrison. Alfred A. Knopf, 1982. ISBN 0-394-84732-6 (ISBN 0-394-94732-0, library binding).

Do you wear braces and hate it? This book tries to make this experience easier by giving you information about how braces work, why you need them, and how to cope with them in such situations as eating and kissing. Nonfiction.

Brooks, Jerome. **The Testing of Charlie Hammelman.** Archway Paperbacks, 1979. ISBN 0-671-29916-6.

Charlie Hammelman is lonely and feels self-conscious about being fat. To make matters worse, he must now face the swimming test required to graduate from school. Then Charlie's favorite teacher dies suddenly, just when he needs her most. Charlie wonders how he can go on without this teacher's help. Fiction.

Childress, Alice. **Rainbow Jordan.** Flare Books, 1982. ISBN 0-380-58974-5.

Fourteen-year-old Rainbow Jordan knows that her irresponsible mother does not care for her. Pushed in and out of a temporary foster home, Rainbow also faces pressure from friends who want her to grow up too fast. Rainbow realizes she must stand up to her friends and also face the truth about her mother, even though both tasks will be painful. Fiction.

Colman, Hila. **Accident.** William Morrow & Co., 1980. ISBN 0-688-22238-2 (ISBN 0-688-32238-7, library binding). Archway Paperbacks, 1981 (paperback). ISBN 0-671-43106-4.

Fifteen-year-old Jenny is the lovely daughter of a bartender. She becomes attracted to wealthy, college-bound Adam. On their first date, however, Jenny is thrown from his motorcycle and paralyzed. From this point on, life becomes a continuous struggle for Jenny as she fights social class prejudices and her own depression. Fiction.

Colman, Hila. **Ellie's Inheritance.** William Morrow & Co., 1979. ISBN 0-688-22204-8. ISBN 0-688-32204-2 (library binding).

When her father loses the family fortune during the 1930s, Ellie, a Jewish girl from New York, leaves college to take a job. Then

Ellie falls in love with a young political radical. She soon finds herself forced to a new maturity by the tragedy that surrounds their relationship. Fiction.

Danziger, Paula. **Can You Sue Your Parents for Malpractice?** Delacorte Press, 1981. ISBN 0-440-01050-0.

Lauren's problems at fourteen are overwhelming: a boyfriend who has left her for a cheerleader, a mother who has let her down, her attraction to a "younger man" (eighth-grade Zach), and a harsh father who has cut off all ties with Lauren's sister for living with her boyfriend. Filled with humor and pain, Lauren's life has some surprises in store for her. Fiction.

Danziger, Paula. **There's a Bat in Bunk Five.** Delacorte Press, 1980. ISBN 0-440-08605-1 (ISBN 0-440-08606-X, library binding).

Working at a summer camp is a wild experience for fifteen-year-old Marcy. She has to deal with her slightly nutty teacher, Ms. Finney. She tries to reach Ginger, a problem camper. And she falls in love with Ted. The summer quickly becomes a series of touching and funny events for Marcy. Fiction.

Davidson, Mary S. **A Superstar Called Sweetpea.** Viking Press, 1980. ISBN 0-670-68478-3.

Elizabeth Barrett wants so much to become a rock star that she lies to her parents and her boyfriend in order to join a high school rock band. With help from her friends, Elizabeth manages to keep her double life a secret. Then the situation becomes too complicated, and Elizabeth must decide whether her singing career is really the most important thing in her life. Fiction.

Degens, T. **Friends.** Viking Press, 1981. ISBN 0-670-33051-5.

How could her mother run away? Eleven-year-old Elinor Atwood pretends to accept her mother's desertion, but inside she is full of anger, hate, and confusion. An older friend tries to help Elinor understand her emotions and face the reality of her mother's action. Fiction.

Delton, Jina. **Two Blocks Down.** Signet Vista Books, 1982. ISBN 0-451-11477-9.

When sixteen-year-old Star moves from the city to the suburbs, she thinks she has nothing in common with any of the people in her new school. Her real friends seem to be back in the city at the

Vagary, a club where the college crowd meets. But then Star makes some new friends and decides to introduce them to her old friends at the Vagary. Star really does not expect the tension and troubles that arise when these two groups meet. Fiction.

Dragonwagon, Crescent, and Paul Zindel. **To Take a Dare.** Harper & Row, Publishers, 1982. ISBN 0-06-026858 (ISBN 0-06-026859-X, library binding).

Two years after thirteen-year-old Chrysta runs away from an abusive father and an obese mother, she finds herself in Excelsior Springs, Arkansas. There she becomes involved with Dare, a homeless boy who reminds Chrysta of her younger self, and Luke, who loves her in spite of her past. Mature language and situations. Fiction.

Dryden, Pamela. **Mask for My Heart.** Signet Vista Books, 1982. ISBN 0-451-11943-6.

When shy sixteen-year-old Cindy McLain meets popular Chris Porter at a masquerade ball, she does not suspect the encounter will force her into living and juggling three separate lives. Pressures mount until a series of events makes Cindy realize she must be honest with herself and others. Fiction.

Francis, Dorothy B. **Captain Morgana Mason.** Lodestar Books, 1982. ISBN 0-525-66764-4.

Morgana Mason lives with her grandfather in Florida. She is only thirteen when he becomes too sick to work. Morgana and her brother Seth take over the family sponge business and try to hold the family together so they won't have to live with their mother, who deserted them. During the summer, Morgana learns as much about herself and life as she does about hooking sponges and sailing. Fiction.

French, Dorothy Kayser. **I Don't Belong Here.** Hiway Books, 1980. ISBN 0-664-32664-1.

The last place senior Mary Glass wants to be is with her grandmother—especially when her parents are going to be in South America. Gram is unpredictable, moody, and forgetful, and Mary does not know how to handle her. Then an accident puts Gram in the hospital, and Mary decides to rethink her relationship with her grandmother. Fiction.

Gaeddert, LouAnn. **Just like Sisters.** Illus. Gail Owens. E. P. Dutton, 1981. ISBN 0-525-32959-5.

Carrie Clark is unprepared for the meanness of her cousin Kate, who comes to visit during the summer Kate's parents decide to get a divorce. Carrie and Kate argue, and Kate runs away. Carrie wonders if she hasn't been wrong about Kate all along. Fiction.

Gerber, Merrill Joan. **Please Don't Kiss Me Now.** Signet Vista Books, 1982. ISBN 0-451-11575-9.

After her parents' divorce, fifteen-year-old Leslie struggles to understand her mother's new life-style and her father's new wife and family. Feeling hurt and rejected, Leslie turns to her music, and then to Brian, the most popular boy in school. But neither music nor Brian seems to help much. Just when her life seems totally out of control, a sudden tragedy makes Leslie see her situation in a new way. Fiction.

Gilbert, Sara. **How to Live with a Single Parent.** Lothrop, Lee & Shepard Books, 1982. ISBN 0-688-00633-7 (ISBN 0-688-00587-X, paperback).

This book offers sound and practical advice to the nearly six million American teenagers who live with a single parent. There are discussions of money, trouble between parents, anger, fear, and single parents' life-styles. Nonfiction.

Gilbert, Sara. **Trouble at Home.** Lothrop, Lee & Shepard Books, 1981. ISBN 0-688-41995-X.

This book describes the kinds of family crises in which teenagers often find themselves and suggests what teenagers can do to survive these tense situations. The book recommends that teenagers recognize and express the emotions that result from serious family problems, not keep them bottled up inside. Nonfiction.

Gilson, Jamie. **Do Bananas Chew Gum?** Lothrop, Lee & Shepard Books, 1980. ISBN 0-688-41960-7 (ISBN 0-688-51960-1, library binding). Archway Paperbacks, 1981 (paperback). ISBN 0-671-42690-7.

Sam Mott is in the sixth grade before anyone discovers he has a learning disability—he cannot read as well as most second-graders. Now Sam must be tested and get special help so that something can be done about his problem. Fiction.

Girion, Barbara. **A Tangle of Roots.** Charles Scribner's Sons, 1979. ISBN 0-684-16074-9.

Sixteen-year-old Beth Frankle's life revolves around her school work, her family, her boyfriend, and her social life. But then her mother's sudden and unexpected death throws her into a dark confusion of fear, anger, and grief. Beth, her father, and her mother's family are now left to rearrange their lives and their relationships while they struggle with their loss and pain. Fiction.

Greene, Shep. **The Boy Who Drank Too Much.** Viking Press, 1979. ISBN 0-670-18381-4.

Buff Sanders, at fourteen, is a new boy in school and a star hockey player. The story, told by his teammate, describes Buff's two major problems: his own drinking and a demanding alcoholic father who beats Buff and pressures the boy to achieve excellence in sports. Fiction.

Hall, Lynn. **The Leaving.** Charles Scribner's Sons, 1980. ISBN 0-684-16716-6. Tempo Books, 1983 (paperback). ISBN 0-441-47776-3.

Roxanne Armstrong decides to leave her beloved rural farm after high school graduation to try city life in Des Moines. What she cannot foresee is that her decision to leave home will cause great changes in her own life and will also affect her parents' lives. Fiction.

Hansen, Joyce. **Home Boy.** Clarion Books, 1982. ISBN 0-89919-114-2.

When Marcus's parents brought him from their island home in the Caribbean to New York City, they thought life would be better for their teenage son. But pressures of the inner city, including drugs and violence, begin to overwhelm Marcus. Fiction.

Hautzig, Deborah. **Second Star to the Right.** Flare Books, 1982. ISBN 0-380-60343-8.

Fourteen-year-old Leslie Hiller's case of anorexia nervosa lands her in a special hospital ward when she nearly starves herself to death. Now Leslie must slowly learn to overcome her emotional problems in order to live a normal life again. Fiction.

Heck, Bessie Holland. **Golden Arrow.** Illus. Charles Robinson. Charles Scribner's Sons, 1981. ISBN 0-684-16882-0.

Thirteen-year-old Randy Colson works all summer on his grandfather's farm to earn money for a motorcycle. But when Golden

Arrow, a palomino colt, is born, Randy abandons his career choice of professional motorcycling in favor of operating a palomino ranch. Now he dreads telling his dad about his new plans. Fiction.

Heide, Florence Parry. **The Wendy Puzzle.** Holiday House, 1982. ISBN 0-8234-0463-3.

Dodie's sister Wendy ruins life for everyone with her constant yelling and sour attitude. Then Dodie discovers torn fragments of poetry and realizes that Wendy's obsession with ecology and her love for the earth have changed Wendy forever. Fiction.

Herman, Charlotte. **What Happened to Heather Hopkowitz?** E. P. Dutton, 1981. ISBN 0-525-42455-5.

Fourteen-year-old Heather Kopkowitz reluctantly visits an orthodox Jewish family while her parents are on vacation. Once there, she is forced to reexamine her old ideas about religion and her relationship to it. Soon Heather realizes the experience is changing her for good. Fiction.

Jones, Rebecca C. **Angie and Me.** Macmillan Publishing Co., 1981. ISBN 0-02-747980-3.

Coping with juvenile rheumatoid arthritis is a painful, frightening experience for twelve-year-old Jenna. In the hospital, she meets Angie, a longtime hospital patient whose courage and wit help them both face their troubles. Fiction.

Kaplow, Robert. **Two in the City.** Houghton Mifflin Co., 1979. ISBN 0-395-27813-9.

High school senior David Riddle rejects his parents' plans for his college education so that he and his girlfriend, Stacey, can move to Greenwich Village and live in an apartment of their own. There, caught between their love and the pressures of finding jobs, living in the city, and adjusting to one another, David and Stacey find their relationship seriously threatened. Mature situations. Fiction.

Kerr, M. E. **What I Really Think of You.** Harper & Row, Publishers, 1982. ISBN 0-06-023188-2 (ISBN 0-06-023189-0, library binding).

Opal Ringer, the sixteen-year-old daughter of a popular preacher of the Helping Hand Tabernacle, has to struggle with her self-image. She also must deal with her feelings for Jesse Pegler, the son of a well-known, flashy television evangelist. Although their families and faiths cause them to live in very different worlds, Opal and Jesse discover common ground upon which to build a relationship. Fiction.

Krementz, Jill. **How It Feels to Be Adopted.** Alfred A. Knopf, 1982. ISBN 0-394-52851-4.

This book allows us to share the emotions and experiences of nineteen adopted children between the ages of eight and sixteen. These children tell us of their thoughts about natural and adopted brothers and sisters, the reactions of friends to adoption, and their own feelings about their situations. In addition, some of the children talk about their relationships with their "birthparents." Each interview is accompanied by a picture of the child with his or her adopted family. Nonfiction.

Krementz, Jill. **How It Feels When a Parent Dies.** Alfred A. Knopf, 1981. ISBN 0-394-51911-6.

Here are stories of young people, from seven to sixteen years old, who have experienced the death of a parent. These young people talk freely and honestly about their pain, confusion, anger, and guilt at their loss. Included are photographs of each child at home with the surviving parent, brothers and sisters, and pets. Nonfiction.

Laiken, Deidre S., and Alan J. Schneider. **Listen to Me, I'm Angry.** Illus. Bernice Myers. Lothrop, Lee & Shepard Books, 1980. ISBN 0-688-41943-7.

Anger is a normal, healthy emotion. This book explores the nature of anger and offers techniques to teenagers for accepting anger and using it constructively. Nonfiction.

Lipsyte, Robert. **The Summerboy.** Harper & Row, Publishers, 1982. ISBN 0-06-023888-7 (ISBN 0-06-023889-5, library binding).

Eighteen-year-old Bobby Marks finds a summer job in a laundry. There he is involved in an exciting struggle for safer working conditions for employees, and he also helps a friend get through an abortion. Fiction.

Lorimer, L. T. **Secrets.** Holt, Rinehart & Winston, 1981. ISBN 0-03-059049-3.

Maggie is only sixteen when her world is shaken by the growing suspicion that her minister father has a secret life of his own that is taking him away from his family and his church. Shocked and hurt, Maggie can only sit back and watch. What happens teaches her the values of honesty—even if it means pain. Fiction.

Mazer, Norma Fox. **Mrs. Fish, Ape, and Me, the Dump Queen.** E. P. Dutton, 1980. ISBN 0-525-35380-1.

Joyce is teased by the kids at school because her uncle, Old Dad, runs the town dump. Life only becomes bearable again after she meets Mrs. Fish, the school custodian. Things become even more fascinating when Mrs. Fish meets Old Dad. Fiction.

Mazer, Norma Fox. **Up in Seth's Room.** Delacorte Press, 1979. ISBN 0-440-08920-4.

Finn is a fifteen-year-old girl who is learning to cope with her growing sexuality. She is determined to see Seth, despite her parents' disapproval. But she is equally determined to maintain her standards of behavior, despite Seth's attempts to pressure her. Mature situations. Fiction.

Miller, Sandy. **Smart Girl.** Signet Vista Books, 1982. ISBN 0-451-11887-1.

High school senior Elizabeth Clark is thrilled when a popular boy asks her out. But when she finds out that he asked her because he needs help with his schoolwork, she loses faith in her own attractiveness and decides she will never be used again. Then a new boy in her physics class asks her out. Elizabeth finds herself facing her old fears and wonders if she should ever trust anyone again. Fiction.

Moore, Emily. **Just My Luck.** Unicorn Books, 1982. ISBN 0-525-44009-7.

The need to feel special leads ten-year-old Olivia into a scheme to locate a lost dog. With the reward money for the dog, Olivia hopes she will be able to buy her own puppy. Fiction.

Moore, Emily. **Something to Count On.** Unicorn Books, 1980. ISBN 0-525-39595-4.

Ten-year-old Lorraine Maybe is unable to accept her parents' divorce. She feels ignored by her busy mother and causes problems at school. When Lorraine attempts to test her father's love, her mother finally understands just how unhappy Lorraine is. Fiction.

Morton, Jane. **Running Scared.** Elsevier/Nelson Books, 1979. ISBN 0-525-66631-1.

Fifteen-year-old Dave Miller's life is not easy. He can't get along with his father and he can't read. Then Dave steals a car and gets sent to Juvenile Hall. There he meets Pat, a counselor. Taking advantage of Dave's love of running, Pat encourages Dave to join the school track team, in the hope that Dave's success in sports will help in other areas of his life. Fiction.

Mulligan, Kevin. **Kid Brother.** Lothrop, Lee & Shepard Books, 1982. ISBN 0-688-00896-8. Tempo Books, 1983 (paperback). ISBN 0-441-43732-X.

Fifteen-year-old Brad finds it difficult to compete with his popular, talented older brother. But a summer in New Mexico with his offbeat aunt gives Brad new confidence in himself and his musical abilities. Mature language. Fiction.

Newton, Suzanne. **M. V. Sexton Speaking.** Viking Press, 1981. ISBN 0-670-44505-3.

Sixteen-year-old Martha Venable Sexton's summer job at a bakery provides her with humorous experiences, love, and some new ideas about herself. Soon Martha even gains the courage to ask her strict aunt for the real story about her dead parents. Fiction.

O'Dell, Scott. **The Spanish Smile.** Houghton Mifflin Co., 1982. ISBN 0-395-32867-5.

Beautiful Lucinda's father has kept her a pampered prisoner in his island castle. However, when the outside world enters her enchanted island, Lucinda learns some horrifying truths about her father. Fiction.

Okimoto, Jean Davies. **It's Just Too Much.** Archway Paperbacks, 1982. ISBN 0-671-43492-6.

Cynthia Browne's world is drastically changed when her mother remarries. Not only does she have to deal with changes in her personal life, but she has to do it with two new stepbrothers around. Fiction.

Okimoto, Jean Davies. **My Mother Is Not Married to My Father.** Archway Paperbacks, 1981. ISBN 0-671-56079-4.

When eleven-year-old Cynthia's parents get divorced and begin new lives as single people, Cynthia and her younger sister, Sara, find themselves confused. Now everyone has to change their lifestyles and their relationships with each other. Fiction.

Oneal, Zibby. **The Language of Goldfish.** Viking Press, 1980. ISBN 0-670-41785-8.

Carrie Stokes wants to remain young forever. At thirteen, she feels trapped between the innocence of childhood and the frightening possibilities of adolescence. In desperation, Carrie attempts suicide. Through therapy, Carrie hopes to learn to accept the idea of growing up. Fiction.

Oppenheimer, Joan L. **Gardine vs. Hanover.** Thomas Y. Crowell Co., 1982. ISBN 0-690-04190-X (ISBN 0-690-4191-8, library binding).

Jill Gardine, fifteen, and Caroline Hanover, sixteen, begin fighting a domestic war after their parents marry and they become stepsisters. Because of their differences, Jill and Caroline come close to destroying the new family their parents are trying to create. Fiction.

Park, Barbara. **Don't Make Me Smile.** Alfred A. Knopf, 1981. ISBN 0-394-84978-7 (ISBN 0-394-94978-1, library binding).

Ten-year-old Charlie Hickle cannot accept his parents' decision to get a divorce. In fact, he would rather live in a tree than with only one parent. Charlie decides to change the situation, but he really only succeeds in changing himself. Fiction.

Pascal, Francine. **The Hand-Me-Down Kid.** Viking Press, 1980. ISBN 0-670-35969-6.

Eleven-year-old Ari Jacobs feels the disadvantages of being the youngest child. All she seems to get are hand-me-downs, teasing, and abuse from her brother and sister. Then an unexpected series of events shakes up the Jacobs family and allows Ari to come out on top for once. Fiction.

Perl, Lila. **Don't Ask Miranda.** Seabury Press, 1979. ISBN 0-8164-3229-5.

When Miranda's parents move to Long Island, New York, she feels lonely and lost in yet another new school. At thirteen she wants friends badly. But she wonders if she wants them badly enough to lie and steal during a class election campaign. Fiction.

Perl, Lila. **Hey, Remember Fat Glenda?** Clarion Books, 1981. ISBN 0-395-31023-7.

Tired of being called "Jelly Belly," Glenda is determined to lose weight. Her mother, a compulsive snacker, is little help, and

Glenda herself occasionally sneaks an extra snack or two. But her crush on Mr. Hartley, the eighth-grade English teacher, inspires her to keep dieting and to audition for the talent review. Fiction.

Pevsner, Stella. **Cute Is a Four-Letter Word.** Clarion Books, 1980. ISBN 0-395-29106-2. Archway Paperbacks, 1981 (paperback). ISBN 0-671-42208-1.

As she starts eighth grade, Clara looks forward to making the Pom Pom Team and winning Skip, the basketball captain. But all her goals may be ruined by snooty Halycyon and her friends Angel and Fergy. Fiction.

Pfeffer, Susan Beth. **What Do You Do When Your Mouth Won't Open?** Illus. Lorna Tomei. Delacorte Press, 1981. ISBN 0-440-09471-2 (ISBN 0-440-09475-5, library binding).

Winning a junior high essay contest is a thrill for Reesa until she finds out she has to read the essay out loud in front of five hundred people. It takes some drastic measures for Reesa to overcome her phobia about public speaking and face an audience. Fiction.

Pollock, Bruce. **It's Only Rock and Roll.** Houghton Mifflin Co., 1980. ISBN 0-395-29182-8.

Eugene Maybloom finds fame and excitement when he becomes a popular rock 'n' roll performer right after he finishes high school. But his popularity fades quickly, and now Eugene must try to adjust to a new life and new goals. Fiction.

Prince, Alison. **The Turkey's Nest.** William Morrow & Co., 1980. ISBN 0-688-22224-2.

Teenage Kate discovers she's pregnant. She is determined to keep the baby, but she does not want to marry its father. So Kate leaves London to live on a farm with her aunt, and there she discovers a new meaning and purpose for her life. Mature situations. Fiction.

Rhue, Morton. **The Wave.** Laurel-Leaf Books, 1981. ISBN 0-440-99371-7.

When a group of high school students begins to study Nazism in history class, they decide to try an experiment in group pressure. But soon the "experiment" becomes real and threatens the entire student body. This story is based on a real-life incident at a Palo Alto, California, high school. Fiction.

Sachs, Marilyn. **A Summer's Lease.** E. P. Dutton, 1979. ISBN 0-525-40480-5.

Gloria is a talented, competitive fifteen-year-old writer who is filled with ambition. She is especially jealous of the boy who is her coeditor on the school magazine. But when they spend a summer together in the country with their English teacher and several children, Gloria finds herself becoming more accepting of herself and other people. Fiction.

Sampson, Fay. **The Watch on Patterick Fell.** Greenwillow Books, 1980. ISBN 0-688-80261-3.

Roger's father is the director of Patterick Fell, a nuclear power plant that stores a large part of the world's nuclear wastes. When demonstrators protest the plant, Roger and his family are forced to move and assume new identities. Fiction.

Savitz, Harriet May. **If You Can't Be the Sun, Be a Star.** Signet Vista Books, 1982. ISBN 0-451-11755-7.

Sixteen-year-old Candy Miller decides to take on the world when she finally becomes disgusted with the rundown condition of her school and her neighborhood. But except for her new boyfriend, nobody else seems interested in Candy's campaign. Fiction.

Savitz, Harriet May. **Run, Don't Walk.** Signet Vista Books, 1980. ISBN 0-451-09421-2.

Samantha Anderson is just one of the gang until a diving accident in her senior year leaves her paralyzed from the waist down. Suddenly, fighting for the rights of the handicapped becomes important to Samantha. She also becomes interested in Johnny Jay, a fellow wheelchair student at Scot High. Fiction.

Savitz, Harriet May. **Wait until Tomorrow.** Signet Books, 1981. ISBN 0-451-09780-7.

After his mother dies, sixteen-year-old Shawn Blake can see little reason to live. When a suicide attempt fails, Shawn goes to live with his grandfather in an ocean resort town. There he meets and falls in love with Robin, but he does not share her strong opposition to nuclear weapons. This conflict and Shawn's efforts to help his grandfather learn to talk again teach Shawn new lessons about love and life. Fiction.

Schotter, Roni. **A Matter of Time.** Tempo Books, 1981. ISBN 0-448-17274-7.

For sixteen-year-old Lisl Gilbert, facing the idea that her mother is dying from cancer is not as difficult as facing what she believes are her own limitations. But though Lisl loses much when her mother dies, she gains some self-respect and a desire to continue her own life. Fiction.

Slepian, Jan. **The Alfred Summer.** Macmillan Publishing Co., 1980. ISBN 0-02-782920-0.

The task of building a boat brings together four special children: Lester and Alfred, both handicapped, and Myron and Claire, both going through personal problems. It is Alfred who really binds the group emotionally when a near tragedy strikes him. As they respond to this, the children discover their own abilities and values. Fiction.

Slepian, Jan. **Lester's Turn.** Macmillan Publishing Co., 1981. ISBN 0-02-782940-5.

Sixteen-year-old Lester, a victim of cerebral palsy, tries to save his retarded friend Alfie from a slow death in a hospital. By doing this, Lester learns how painful it is to become a young adult, especially when you have a handicap. This book is the sequel to *The Alfred Summer.* Fiction.

Spencer, Zane, and Jay Leech. **Branded Runaway.** Hiway Books, 1980. ISBN 0-664-32662-5.

After a childhood of foster homes and court appearances, seventeen-year-old orphan Reese Sims finds that the only alternative to living in a boys' home is to accept an assignment as a counselor to troubled children in a mountain camp. Once there, a near disaster on a mountain slope during a blizzard teaches Reese as much about himself as about physical survival. Fiction.

Stewart, John Craig. **The Last to Know.** Tempo Books, 1981. ISBN 0-448-17003-5.

Spending a summer as a mate on his Uncle Walton's fishing boat, seventeen-year-old Bruce Weaver is puzzled by his uncle's strict and sometimes cruel treatment of him. With the help of his cousin Louise, Bruce learns the true story of the complicated relationships between his mother, his dead father, and Uncle Walton. Fiction.

Stewart, Marjabelle Young. **The Teen Girl's Guide to Social Success.** Signet Vista Books, 1982. ISBN 0-451-11886-3.

Do social situations make you nervous? From boy-girl parties to job interviews, this handbook has helpful information for young women on how to handle almost all topics relating to social skills. Nonfiction.

Strasser, Todd. **Angel Dust Blues.** Laurel-Leaf Books, 1981. ISBN 0-440-90952-X.

Alex Lazar's life takes a turn for the worse when he becomes involved with Michael McDonald and drugs. Then he gets caught selling angel dust to an undercover agent, and his whole future, including his relationship with his new girlfriend, is threatened. Alex decides to change his life, even if it is a struggle. Mature language and situations. Fiction.

Wood, Phyllis Anderson. **Get a Little Lost, Tia.** Signet Books, 1979. ISBN 0-451-09872-2.

Since his mother works full-time and his father is dead, eighteen-year-old Jason spends most of his time and energy helping his thirteen-year-old sister, Tia, stay out of trouble. The situation for both brother and sister seems to improve when Jason meets Celia, but Tia appears to have plans for both of them that neither suspects. Fiction.

Wyatt, Molly. **Kim's Winter.** Signet Vista Books, 1982. ISBN 0-451-11435-3.

Until her parents are killed in a tragic plane crash, seventeen-year-old Kim Carpenter has spent her life roaming the world with them. The idea of settling down in a small New England town with her grandmother doesn't thrill Kim. But soon she realizes she will have to make the adjustment in order to face the future. Fiction.

York, Carol Beach. **Remember Me When I Am Dead.** Elsevier/Nelson Books, 1980. ISBN 0-525-66694-X.

After nine-year-old Jenny Loring's mother dies in an accident, her father remarries. Jenny has trouble adjusting to the loss of her mother and to her new stepmother. Christmas is hard for Jenny—especially when she receives a gift from her dead mother.

SCIENCE

Adler, David A. **Hyperspace! Facts and Fun from All Over the Universe.** Illus. Fred Winkowski. Viking Press, 1982. ISBN 0-670-38908-0 (ISBN 0-670-05117-9, paperback).

Here is a mixture of facts, puzzles, questions, riddles, projects, and games that will help you learn about the moon, space flight, meteors, planets, asteroids, the sun, the earth, black holes, and much more. Nonfiction.

Atkinson, Linda. **Have We Lived Before?** Illus. Michele Chessare. Dodd, Mead & Co., 1981. ISBN 0-396-07999-7.

In this book, the possibility of rebirth or reincarnation is explored. It begins with a discussion of five famous cases, including the mysterious Bridey Murphy story. The last two chapters, "Is It Possible?" and "Suppose It's True," offer a fair and mind-opening discussion of scientific efforts in this field. Nonfiction.

Bershad, Carol, and Deborah Bernick. **Bodyworks: The Kids' Guide to Food and Physical Fitness.** Illus. Heidi Johanna Selig. Random House, 1981. ISBN 0-394-84752-0 (ISBN 0-394-94752-5, library binding).

Here is a book that can help you improve both your mind and your body. Experiments, exercises, and information about how the body works, physical fitness, and eating habits can help you get into top shape. Originally published as *From the Inside Out.* Nonfiction.

Betancourt, Jeanne. **Am I Normal?** Illus. by author. Flare Books, 1983. ISBN 0-380-82040-4.

Based on an award-winning film, this book discusses the fears, questions, and uncertainties boys face when they reach puberty. Basic information about the male body and about social issues is presented in a clear and direct way. Nonfiction.

Betancourt, Jeanne. **Dear Diary.** Illus. by author. Flare Books, 1983. ISBN 0-380-82057-9.

Here are clear and easy-to-understand answers to common questions girls have about the changes in their bodies during puberty. The book describes and explains the female body and talks about the changing social roles of girls as they move from childhood to young adulthood. Nonfiction.

Cohen, Daniel. **How to Test Your ESP.** Photographs by Joan Men-schenfreund. E. P. Dutton, 1982. ISBN 0-525-45109-9.

This is a book on a subject that people still argue about. It begins with a clear introduction to ESP (extra sensory perception) and then goes on to give stories of people who claim to have various forms of ESP. Each true story includes an explanation of the method used to test the person's particular ESP ability. Nonfiction.

D'Amato, Janet Potter. **Who's a Horn? What's an Antler? Crafts of Bone and Horn.** Photographs by author. Julian Messner, 1982. ISBN 0-671-41975-7.

Deer and cows are two examples of animals with antlers or horns. This book describes the ways that humans throughout history have turned these animal parts into valuable products. The second half of the book gives directions for projects to make with bone and horn, including jewelry, games, and sound instruments. Nonfiction.

Dolan, Edward F., Jr. **The Bermuda Triangle and Other Mysteries of Nature.** Bantam Books, 1981. ISBN 0-553-14824-9.

This book explores three of nature's most fascinating mysteries. What happened to the 100 ships and planes that have disappeared in the Bermuda Triangle since 1945? Do UFOs contain visitors from outer space? Is the Abominable Snowcreature real or a hoax? Nonfiction.

McGrath, Judith. **Pretty Girl: A Guide to Looking Good, Naturally.** Photographs by Bruce Curtis. Illus. Frederic Marvin. Lothrop, Lee & Shepard Books, 1981. ISBN 0-688-00695-7 (ISBN 0-688-00694-9, library binding).

What shampoo is the best for your hair? How does makeup affect a person's skin? This well-illustrated book provides clear answers and advice for a number of important questions on diet, skin, hair, and body care for teenage girls. Nonfiction.

Nance, John. **Lobo of the Tasaday.** Photographs by author. Pantheon Books, 1982. ISBN 0-394-85007-7.

This is the exciting story of a young boy who belongs to a recently discovered tribe in a remote jungle in the Philippines. Lobo's tribe still lives as people did in the Stone Age, using crude tools and weapons to provide themselves with fire, food, and shelter. Nonfiction.

Nestor, Wiliam P. **Into Winter: Discovering a Season.** Illus. Susan
Banta. Houghton Mifflin Co., 1982. ISBN 0-395-32866-7.

Winter is a season when most people seek comfort indoors. But
there is a great deal to be learned about nature during these cold
months. This book provides information about what to look for
when you explore for plants, mammals, birds, insects, and other
living things in the winter. A number of nature projects for the
winter months are explained in detail. Nonfiction.

Phillips, Betty Lou. **Brush Up on Hair Care.** Illus. Lois Johnson.
Julian Messner, 1982. ISBN 0-671-43852-2.

This is a complete hair care guide for teenagers. It includes information about the physical structure of hair as well as advice
on how to care for your hair and different ways to cut and style it.
Nonfiction.

Rahn, Joan Elma. **Plants Up Close.** Houghton Mifflin Co., 1981. ISBN
0-395-31677-4.

Do you take plants for granted? You won't after you read this
book. Five different plants—tulip, sugar maple, butternut squash,
sunflower, and rose of Sharon—are closely examined here. These
plants are used as examples of the many fascinating ways plants
live and reproduce. Nonfiction.

Smith, Howard E., Jr. **Killer Weather: Stories of Great Disasters.** Dodd,
Mead & Co., 1982. ISBN 0-396-08055-3.

Hurricanes, tornados, volcanoes—here are the stories of twelve
great weather disasters and their causes. Details of the destruction
and human suffering that followed these disasters reveal how
helpless humans still are to control nature. Nonfiction.

Woods, Harold, and Geraldine Woods. **The Book of the Unknown.**
Illus. Joe Mathieu. Random House, 1982. ISBN 0-394-85233-8.

There are many questions that are still unanswered by science.
For example, was there a lost continent called Atlantis? Is ESP
real? Can I live to be 150? This book tries to answer these and
other mysteries while also offering more questions to think about.
Nonfiction.

SPORTS

Bunting, Eve. **The Waiting Game.** J. B. Lippincott, 1981. ISBN 0-397-31941-X.

Three high school seniors who are top players on the football team have a special relationship. As they await word on being accepted into college, their friendship is severely tested. Suddenly they find themselves competing with each other. Fiction.

Chiefari, Janet. **Introducing the Drum and Bugle Corps.** Photographs by Ann Hagen Griffiths. Dodd, Mead & Co., 1982. ISBN 0-396-08088-X.

Discover the inside story of being part of a drum and bugle corps—the marching and drill techniques, the parades, and the competitions. In this book, you will learn about the roles of the brass, percussion, and color guard not only through the text, but also from the action photographs. Nonfiction.

Dygard, Thomas J. **Outside Shooter.** William Morrow & Co., 1979. ISBN 0-688-22177-7.

It is hard to believe, but not every basketball team wants a super-star, especially one who demands special treatment. When Deke Warden takes over the coaching of the Bloomfield High School team, he knows he has a problem when the team superstar gets suspended from school. Deke wonders if helping this superstar straighten out will be worth the time and effort. Fiction.

Dygard, Thomas J. **Point Spread.** William Morrow & Co., 1980. ISBN 0-688-22222-6.

Lou's brilliant career in college football and the promise of a professional career are threatened when he finds himself caught in the middle of a gambling scandal. Lou decides to try and handle the problem himself, but he doesn't realize how difficult and dangerous it will be. Fiction.

Dygard, Thomas J. **Quarterback Walk-on.** William Morrow & Co., 1982. ISBN 0-688-01065-2.

Denny Westbrook is a lowly walk-on, fourth-string quarterback in his senior year of college football. So no one, including Denny, expects him to get a chance to prove his value to the team in an important conference game. But that is just what happens in this funny and touching story. Fiction.

Dygard, Thomas J. **Soccer Duel.** William Morrow & Co., 1981. ISBN 0-688-00366-4.

Terry is used to the role of football hero in his high school. But when he decides to play on the soccer team, he meets a talented new teammate from Poland. Now Terry has to struggle with his ego while he learns the new skills of soccer. Fiction.

Fischler, Stan. **More Stan Fischler's Sports Stumpers.** Tempo Books, 1978. ISBN 0-448-16488-4.

What outfielder went from prison to the big leagues? What boxer was nicknamed "The Toy Bulldog"? Find out the answers to these and other questions in Stan Fischler's book for sports addicts of all ages. Nonfiction.

Fremon, David. **Secrets of the Super Athletes: Basketball.** Laurel-Leaf Books, 1982. ISBN 0-440-97647-2.

With tips from basketball greats Bill Russell, Kareem Abdul-Jabbar, Moses Malone, and "Dr. J," you will feel you are getting all the inside secrets about passing, rebounding, dunks, and free throws, as well as valuable advice on training. Included is a special "super athletes quiz." Nonfiction.

Gutman, Bill. **Modern Soccer Superstars.** Dodd, Mead & Co., 1979. ISBN 0-396-07731-5.

The lives of six outstanding professional soccer players are covered from childhood to stardom. These stories are dramatic and instructive as they reveal the hard work, skill, and determination needed to become truly great in sports. Featured are Pelé, Jim McAlister, Kyle Rote, Jr., Werner Roth, Al Trost, and Shep Messing. Nonfiction.

Hollander, Zander, ed. **The Baseball Book.** Random House, 1982. ISBN 0-394-84296-0.

This is an easy A to Z encyclopedia about America's favorite pastime. The material here includes baseball facts, the stories of legendary games, and the achievements of famous players. Photographs are included, as are lists of the all-time records of baseball's most successful athletes. Nonfiction.

Kalb, Jonah, and Laura Kalb. **The Easy Ice Skating Book.** Illus. Sandy Kossin. Houghton Mifflin Co., 1981. ISBN 0-395-31605-7.

Knowing how to fit skates before you try the basic movements is just one thing you will learn by reading this clearly written and illustrated "how-to" book. The advice is designed to help people who have never skated before prepare themselves for their first time on the ice. Nonfiction.

Kaplan, Janice. **First Ride.** Flare Books, 1982. ISBN 0-380-78055-0.

Fourteen-year-old Cadmy Stephens wants to qualify for the National Finals in bull riding. But traveling the rodeo circuit means going against her parents, the other members of her school's rodeo team, and the traditional rodeo prejudice against female competitors. While proving herself, Cadmy learns lessons about human nature and the power of love. Fiction.

Kidd, Ronald. **Dunker.** Lodestar Books, 1982. ISBN 0-525-66762-8.

The parents of sixteen-year-old Bobby want him to be a famous child actor. Bobby, however, would prefer to live life as a regular high school student whose only worries are getting a date and making the basketball team. How will he decide on the best lifestyle? Fiction.

Kidd, Ronald. **Who Is Felix the Great?** Lodestar Books, 1983. ISBN 0-525-66778-4.

The magic of baseball is seen through the eyes of eleventh-grader Tim Julian as he searches for some memories of his father and his baseball idol. What can Tim learn from the story of a once-famous person? Fiction.

Litsky, Frank. **Winners in Gymnastics.** Camelot Books, 1979. ISBN 0-380-43299-4.

Much of this short book contains exciting action photographs of seven world-class gymnasts. The text describes the lives of these sports champions—what made them decide to enter gymnastics and what has made them successful competitors. Nonfiction.

McCrackin, Mark. **A Winning Position.** Photographs by Harold Roth. Laurel-Leaf Books, 1982. ISBN 0-440-99483-7.

Seventeen-year-old Alec does his best to qualify for the regional stock car race, but his personal life needs some attention too. Alec feels torn between pleasing his parents, his girlfriend, and his racing coach. But a surprising incident at the track helps Alec understand the importance of thinking about his future plans and personal relationships. Fiction.

McWhirter, Norris, and Chris Cook. **Guinness Book of Sports Records: Winners and Champions.** Sterling Publishing Co., 1980. ISBN 0-8069-0182-9.

This book discusses men and women who have been successful in team or individual sports. Athletes participating in over seventy sports are included. Pictures and lists of records help show the great competitiveness of these world-class athletes. Nonfiction.

McWhirter, Norris, Steve Morgenstern, Roz Morgenstern, and Stan Greenberg. **Guinness Book of Women's Sports Records.** Sterling Publishing Co., 1979. ISBN 0-8069-0162-4 (ISBN 0-8069-0163-2, library binding).

Through this book you will meet women athletes in over three dozen sports and will discover their records as amateurs and professionals. Their stories of determination, defeat, and success are an inspiration to rising young athletes of both sexes. Nonfiction.

Olney, Ross R. **Modern Speed Record Superstars.** Dodd, Mead & Co., 1982. ISBN 0-396-08072-3.

Speed record superstars are people who like the ultimate challenge: daring death and surviving. This book shows that as soon as someone sets a speed record in a car, cycle, boat, or plane, someone else comes along to try and break that record. The stories of six of these record holders and their daring feats are told here. Photographs. Nonfiction.

Olney, Ross R. **Tricky Discs: Frisbee Saucer Flying.** Lothrop, Lee & Shepard Books, 1979. ISBN 0-688-41891-0 (ISBN 0-688-51891-5, library binding).

Whether you are interested in Frisbee technique for competition or just for a lazy game of toss and catch, this book will provide you with a complete guide to improving your knowledge of this fast-growing sport. Nonfiction.

Olney, Ross R. **Winners! Super Champions of Ice Hockey.** Clarion Books, 1982. ISBN 0-89919-109-6.

Who are the best ice hockey players today? What are they like as athletes and as people? These questions are covered in this illustrated book that also explains how the often-dangerous sport of professional ice hockey is played. Nonfiction.

Quigley, Martin. **The Original Colored House of David.** Houghton Mifflin Co., 1981. ISBN 0-395-31608-1.

In the 1920s, baseball came to small towns in the form of traveling teams. One day, a spectacular black team comes to a certain town. Seventeen-year-old Timothy knows he is the best player in town, so he convinces the black team to take him along on their tour as a relief player. But in order to do this, white Timothy must pretend to be a deaf-mute albino! Fiction.

Ryan, Frank. **Jumping for Joy.** Illus. Elizabeth T. Hall. Charles Scribner's Sons, 1980. ISBN 0-684-16337-3.

The history of pole vaulting and the development of styles in the high jump, long jump, and triple jump are discussed in this informative book. It also gives helpful advice for those who want to develop their jumping skills. Nonfiction.

Slote, Alfred. **The Hotshot.** Photographs by William LaCrosse. Laurel-Leaf Books, 1979. ISBN 0-440-93706-X.

Paddy O'Neill was determined to show off his talents and make it on the all-city basketball team. But instead of playing a team game, Paddy tries to get the glory shots himself. As a result, he causes his team to lose. Will this lesson be enough to teach Paddy the importance of teamwork? Fiction.

Sullivan, George. **The Art of Base-Stealing.** Dodd, Mead & Co., 1982. ISBN 0-396-08040-5.

The best teams in baseball today can boast two or three "bandits" —players who can easily steal a base. This book discusses a few of these skillful runners while it gives some tips about base-stealing. A section filled with statistics and records is also provided. Photographs. Nonfiction.

Thorn, John. **Baseball's Ten Greatest Games.** Four Winds Press, 1981. ISBN 0-590-07665-5.

Batter up! Beginning with the Detroit Tigers vs. the Philadelphia A's in 1907, and continuing up through the New York Yankees vs. the Boston Red Sox in 1978, this book covers the ten most exciting games in baseball. Several full-page photographs and a list of statistics for each of these games add interest to the stories. Nonfiction.

Thorn, John. **Pro Football's Ten Greatest Games.** Four Winds Press, 1981. ISBN 0-590-07788-0.

The ten best football games of the past fifty years are brought to life in this book. Detailed diagrams, action photographs, and statistics for each game help make the material even more interesting and informative. Nonfiction.

Wallace, Barbara Brooks. **Hawkins and the Soccer Solution.** Illus. Gloria Kamen. Abingdon Press, 1981. ISBN 0-687-16672-1.

Harvey and his buddies are ready for soccer season, but they have lost their sponsor. And without a sponsor, the team has no money to buy uniforms and equipment. With the help of Hawkins, a clever friend, the team finds a new sponsor and even comes up with humorous plans for improving their game. Fiction.

THE SUPERNATURAL

Bunting, Eve. **The Ghosts of Departure Point.** J. B. Lippincott Co., 1982. ISBN 0-397-31997-5.

Vicki and Ted, teenage ghosts, meet at the scene of the accident where they were both killed. As they begin to care for each other, they realize that there is a way they can make up for their own deaths and the deaths of their friends. Fiction.

Clifford, Eth. **The Strange Reincarnations of Hendrik Verloom.** Houghton Mifflin Co., 1982. ISBN 0-395-32433-5.

Fourteen-year-old Anna is determined to find out who has been playing jokes on the people in her apartment building. She is also determined to find out about her grandfather's previous lives. Has he really been reincarnated? Fiction.

Cohen, Daniel. **Famous Curses.** Archway Paperbacks, 1981. ISBN 0-671-41867-X.

Both facts and opinions about ten famous curses calling for bad luck, injury, or death are given in this book. It is up to the reader to decide—do curses really work? Photographs. Nonfiction.

Cohen, Daniel. **Ghostly Terrors.** Dodd, Mead & Co., 1981. ISBN 0-396-07996-2.

Want some great stories for a stormy night? Here are thirteen ghostly tales—reported to be true—about haunted castles, missing corpses, and people buried alive. Photographs. Nonfiction.

Cohen, Daniel. **The Headless Roommate and Other Tales of Terror.** Illus. Peggy Brier. Bantam Books, 1982. ISBN 0-553-20382-7.

This is a collection of frightening and occasionally funny horror stories. All are modern—you may have heard of some of them at late-night campfires and slumber parties. Fiction.

Cohen, Daniel. **Real Magic.** Dodd, Mead & Co., 1982. ISBN 0-396-08095-2.

You have probably seen "stage magic"—tricks and illusions performed in theaters and on TV. Here is a book about "real magic" involving the supernatural—the "Indian rope trick," Houdini's "return from the dead," voodoo, alchemy, and spell casting. Photographs. Nonfiction.

Cohen, Daniel. **The World's Most Famous Ghosts.** Archway Paperbacks, 1979. ISBN 0-671-43683-X.

Here are stories about famous ghosts. Some of the stories are easily explained, but a number of these events remain unexplained. Are ghosts real? After reading these tales, you must decide for yourself. Photographs. Nonfiction.

Coontz, Otto. **The Night Walkers.** Houghton Mifflin Co., 1982. ISBN 0-395-32557-9.

No one will believe that the children of Covendale are possessed by an evil spirit—the spirit of darkness. Once the spirit has breathed into them, they become night walkers, seeking others to add to their numbers. Thirteen-year-old Nora discovers the cause of this horrifying plague and its cure. But can she help the people in her town before she becomes one of the night walkers? Fiction.

Duncan, Lois. **A Gift of Magic.** Archway Paperbacks, 1981. ISBN 0-671-83242-5.

Twelve-year-old Nancy, who has ESP, is unhappy about her parents' divorce and the changes in her family. But as she comes to accept her new life, she also learns how to use her gift wisely. Fiction.

Furman, A. L., editor. **Ghost Stories.** Archway Paperbacks, 1978. ISBN 0-671-29922-0.

Here are eerie tales from eight authors. In these stories you will find terror and adventure in a cave, a castle, the Scottish Highlands, and the American West. Fiction.

Hahn, Mary Downing. **The Time of the Witch.** Clarion Books, 1982. ISBN 0-89919-115-0.

Laura and her little brother spend the summer in West Virginia after their parents separate. Laura tells an old woman of her wish for her parents to get back together—without realizing the woman is a real witch. Fiction.

Hoppe, Joanne. **April Spell.** Archway Paperbacks, 1982. ISBN 0-671-43869-7.

Jennie Littleton visits Palmer Memorial Church in her Connecticut hometown as part of a school assignment. But her life is never the same after attending services in the "ghost church." How can Jennie not believe in ghosts now? Fiction.

Swearingen, Martha. **If Anything.** Elsevier/Nelson Books, 1980. ISBN 0-525-66673-7.

The ghost of Martin Evans, a lonely young man, slowly and unwillingly falls in love with the ghost of Ashgrove. Ashgrove comes to love Martin—but she also loves her house, which she died for and now happily haunts. Can these ghosts stay together? Fiction.

York, Carol Beach. **Revenge of the Dolls.** Elsevier/Nelson Books, 1979. ISBN 0-525-66632-X.

Aunt Sarah is mad but harmless—at least, that's what the grown-ups think. But Alice knows better. She and her sister, Trissy, know about the evil dolls that talk to their aunt. And Alice knows about the doll Aunt Sarah makes to get even with cousin Paulie. Fiction.

York, Carol Beach. **When Midnight Comes. . . .** Elsevier/Nelson Books, 1979. ISBN 0-525-66676-1.

At first Joan thinks her mother, little sister, and brother changed because cousin Wilma was visiting. But they still act strangely after Wilma goes home. What is really causing the changes? Could it be related to what is haunting the house? Fiction.

TRIVIA

Anderson, Doug. **Eye Spy.** Sterling Publishing Co., 1980. ISBN 0-8069-4628-8 (ISBN 0-8069-4629-6, library binding).

This collection of picture puzzles tests the reader's powers of observation and memory. You will find hours of brain-teasing fun here. Nonfiction.

Aylward, Jim. **You're Dumber in the Summer: And Over 100 Other Things No One Ever Told You.** Illus. Jane Chambless-Rigie. Holt, Rinehart & Winston, 1980. ISBN 0-03-043551-X.

Did you know that you share your birthday with about nine million other people in the world? Or that if you grew as fast as a baby whale, you'd be sixty-five feet tall at age two? Or that a hog can run at a top speed of eleven miles per hour? If you want interesting bits of information, plus humorous illustrations, this book will provide them. Nonfiction.

Boyd, L. M. **Boyd's Book of Odd Facts.** Illus. Alex Chin. Sterling Publishing Co., 1979. ISBN 0-8069-0166-7 (ISBN 0-8069-0167-5, library binding).

Want to know some really odd facts? This is not a routine trivia book with simple lists of information. Here you learn that black sheep have a sharper sense of smell than white sheep have. Or that there are about 550 hairs in a typical eyebrow. Who knows? Maybe reading this book will make *you odd.* Nonfiction.

Brandreth, Gyles. **Seeing Is Not Believing.** Sterling Publishing Co., 1980. ISBN 0-8069-4614-8 (ISBN 0-8069-4615-6, library binding).

This collection of optical illusions will make you doubt your own eyes. It might *not* be a good idea to read this straight through—unless you want to recapture the feeling of spinning in a tree swing after the ropes are twisted tightly! Nonfiction.

Fortunato, Pat. **Advice from the Superstars.** Bantam Books, 1982. ISBN 0-553-15128-2.

If you want to hear some serious and humorous advice from some of your favorite stars, this book is for you. Dr. J., Chevy Chase, Donny Osmond, Andy Gibb, and others answer questions about family, friends, feelings, sports, school, and much more. Photographs. Nonfiction.

Paraguin, Charles H. **Eye Teasers: Optical Illusion Puzzles.** Illus. by author. Sterling Publishing Co., 1980. ISBN 0-8069-4538-9 (ISBN 0-8069-4539-7, library binding).

Here is a book you can read straight through or just dip into. You will find many kinds of optical illusions, from visual impossibilities and afterimages to hidden objects. Nonfiction.

SERIES BOOKS

Alfred Hitchcock Mystery Series and The Three Investigators Mystery Series

The Three Investigators—Jupiter Jones, Bob Andrews, and Pete Crenshaw—work out of their mobile home headquarters in the Jones Salvage Yard to solve mysteries and crimes that baffle the adult detectives. In many of the books they are joined by Alfred Hitchcock. Random House.

Books by William Arden

Alfred Hitchcock and The Three Investigators in The Mystery of the Dancing Devil. 1981. ISBN 0-394-84862-4.
Alfred Hitchcock and The Three Investigators in The Mystery of the Dead Man's Riddle. 1980. ISBN 0-394-84451-3.
Alfred Hitchcock and The Three Investigators in The Mystery of the Deadly Double. 1981. ISBN 0-394-84491-2.
Alfred Hitchcock and The Three Investigators in The Mystery of the Headless Horse. 1981. ISBN 0-394-84861-6.
Alfred Hitchcock and The Three Investigators in The Secret of the Crooked Cat. 1981. ISBN 0-394-84677-X.
The Three Investigators in The Mystery of the Purple Pirate. 1982. ISBN 0-394-84951-5 (ISBN 0-394-94951-X, library binding).

Book by Robert Arthur

Alfred Hitchcock and The Three Investigators in the Mystery of the Vanishing Treasure. 1980. ISBN 0-394-84452-1.

Books by M. V. Carey

Alfred Hitchcock and The Three Investigators in The Mystery of Death Trap Mine. 1980. ISBN 0-394-84449-1.
Alfred Hitchcock and The Three Investigators in The Mystery of the Invisible Dog. 1981. ISBN 0-394-84492-0.

Alfred Hitchcock and The Three Investigators in The Mystery of the Magic Circle. 1981. ISBN 0-394-84490-4.
Alfred Hitchcock and The Three Investigators in The Mystery of the Singing Serpent. 1981. ISBN 0-394-84678-8.
Alfred Hitchcock and The Three Investigators in The Secret of the Haunted Mirror. 1980. ISBN 0-394-84450-5.
The Three Investigators in The Mystery of the Blazing Cliffs. 1981. ISBN 0-394-84504-8 (ISBN 0-394-94504-2, library binding).
The Three Investigators in The Mystery of the Wandering Cave Man. 1982. ISBN 0-394-85278-8 (ISBN 0-394-95278-2, library binding).

Books by Nick West

Alfred Hitchcock and The Three Investigators in The Mystery of the Coughing Dragon. 1981. ISBN 0-394-84666-4.
Alfred Hitchcock and The Three Investigators in The Mystery of the Nervous Lion. 1981. ISBN 0-394-84665-6.

Audubon Society Beginner Guides

These illustrated guidebooks by George S. Fichter provide an introduction to wildlife, plant life, and natural resources. Tips are given to help you identify what you see as you study nature. And the books are small enough to fit into a pocket, so you can take them along on your nature walks. Random House.

Birds of North America. Illus. Arthur Singer. 1982. ISBN 0-394-84771-7.
Reptiles and Amphibians of North America. Illus. Sy Barlowe. 1982. ISBN 0-394-84769-5.
Rocks and Minerals. Illus. Patricia J. Wynne. 1982. ISBN 0-394-84772-5.
Wildflowers of North America. Illus. Dorothea Barlowe. 1982. ISBN 0-394-84770-9.

The Baker Street Irregulars Series

The Baker Street Irregulars—Dan, Liz, Mickey, and Jeff—combine their talents to solve crimes and mysteries involving ghosts, stolen goods, and firebugs. The series author is Terrance Dicks. A description of each title can be found in the Mystery and Crime section. Elsevier/Nelson Books.

The Baker Street Irregulars in The Case of the Blackmail Boys. 1981. ISBN 0-525-66710-5.
The Baker Street Irregulars in The Case of the Cinema Swindle. 1980. ISBN 0-525-66728-8.

The Baker Street Irregulars in The Case of the Cop Catchers. Lodestar Books, 1982. ISBN 0-525-66765-2.
The Baker Street Irregulars in The Case of the Crooked Kids. 1980. ISBN 0-525-66711-3.
The Baker Street Irregulars in The Case of the Ghost Grabbers. 1981. ISBN 0-525-66729-6.
The Baker Street Irregulars in The Case of the Missing Masterpiece. 1979. ISBN 0-525-66656-7.

Emergency Series

Dudley, Samantha, and Nathaniel are EMTs—emergency medical technicians. Ride along with them as they take part in emergency rescues and work to revive victims of heart attacks or accidents. In the last half of each book, learn more about the tasks and responsibilities of these emergency jobs. The series author is Anabel Dean. Benefic Press.

Emergency Air Ambulance. 1980. ISBN 0-8175-1943-2.
Emergency Ambulance #10. 1980. ISBN 0-8175-1941-6.
Emergency Firefighters. 1980. ISBN 0-8175-1944-0.
Emergency Life Support Unit. 1980. ISBN 0-8175-1942-2.
Emergency Rescue Team. 1980. ISBN 0-8175-1945-9.
Emergency Squad. 1980. ISBN 0-8175-1940-8.

How Did We Find Out Series

Isaac Asimov, a famous science and science-fiction writer, describes scientific discoveries that have given us more information about the solar system, our own planet, and the creatures that live on earth. Illustrator for the series is David Wool. Camelot Books.

How Did We Find Out about Antarctica? 1981. ISBN 0-380-53421-5.
How Did We Find Out about Atoms? 1982. ISBN 0-380-59576-1.
How Did We Find Out about Comets? 1981. ISBN 0-380-53454-1.
How Did We Find Out about Dinosaurs? 1982. ISBN 0-380-59584-2.
How Did We Find Out about Earthquakes? 1981. ISBN 0-380-53462-2.
How Did We Find Out about Energy? 1981. ISBN 0-380-53447-9.
How Did We Find Out about Germs? 1981. ISBN 0-380-53439-8.
How Did We Find Out about Life in the Deep Sea? 1982. ISBN 0-380-59592-3.
How Did We Find Out about Our Human Roots? 1982. ISBN 0-380-59600-8.
How Did We Find Out about Outer Space? 1981. ISBN 0-380-53413-4.
How Did We Find Out about Solar Power? 1982. ISBN 0-380-59618-0.
How Did We Find Out about Volcanoes? 1982. ISBN 0-380-59626-1.

Jem Books

These nonfiction books explore the mystery, courage, and adventure found in real life. The subjects include a group of boys who risked their lives to save Jewish children during World War II, a deaf stunt woman, and ESP. Jem Books.

Abrams, Lawrence F. **Mysterious Powers of the Mind.** 1982. ISBN 0-671-43604-X.

Baldwin, Margaret. **The Boys Who Saved the Children.** 1981. ISBN 0-671-43603-1. (A description of this book can be found in the History section.)

Bunting, Eve. **The Giant Squid.** 1981. ISBN 0-671-43776-3.

Foxglove, Lady. **We've Got the Power: Witches among Us.** 1981. ISBN 0-671-43604-X.

Gardner, Sandra. **Six Who Dared.** 1981. ISBN 0-671-43513-2.

Schoder, Judith. **The Blood Suckers.** 1981. ISBN 0-671-43778-X.

Jody and Jake Mystery Series

Teenage detectives Jody and Jake find themselves involved in dangerous mysteries. Who wants to stop the rock concert—and why? Who burns Mark's house and frames him? Why the unusual demands from the racehorse owner? The series author is Elizabeth Levy. Archway Paperbacks.

The Case of the Counterfeit Racehorse. 1980. ISBN 0-671-29965-4.
The Case of the Fired-up Gang. 1981. ISBN 0-671-41140-3.
The Case of the Frightened Rock Star. 1980. ISBN 0-671-29964-6.
The Case of the Wild River Ride. 1981. ISBN 0-671-41141-1.

Raintree Adventure Series

These books describe the true adventures of men and women who have survived severe accidents, escaped the hazards of the wilderness, or tried to swim from Cuba to Florida. Raintree Publishers.

Black, Susan. **Crash in the Widerness.** Illus. Thomas Buchs. 1980. ISBN 0-8172-1553-0.

McLenighan, Valjean. **Diana: Alone against the Sea.** Illus. Jay Blair. 1980. ISBN 0-8172-1557-3.

Stone, Judith. **Minutes to Live.** Illus. Rob Sauber. 1980. ISBN 0-8172-1563-8.

Tripp, Jenny. **The Man Who Was Left for Dead.** Illus. Charles Shaw. 1980. ISBN 0-8172-1556-5.

Tripp, Jenny. **One Was Left Alive.** Illus. John Burgoyne. 1980. ISBN 0-8172-1555-7.

Wilson, Lionel. **Attack of the Killer Grizzly.** Illus. Scott Zoellick. 1980. ISBN 0-8172-1574-3.

Raintree Literary Classics

Join Huck Finn as he floats on a raft down the Mississippi. Travel far below the surface of the ocean. Help Sherlock Holmes unravel mysteries and solve crimes. These classics are retold in language familiar to today's readers, yet the author's original style and tone remain unchanged. Raintree Publishers.

Brontë, Charlotte (adapted by Diana Stewart). **Jane Eyre.** Illus. Charles Shaw. 1981. ISBN 0-8172-1661-8.

Chaucer, Geoffrey (adapted by Diana Stewart). **The Canterbury Tales.** Illus. Dan Hubrich. 1981. ISBN 0-8172-1666-9.

Dickens, Charles (adapted by Patricia Krapesh). **A Tale of Two Cities.** Illus. Charles Shaw. 1980. ISBN 0-8172-1658-8.

Doyle, Sir Arthur Conan (adapted by Diana Stewart). **Sherlock Holmes: Selected Stories.** Illus. Dan Toht. 1980. ISBN 0-8172-1657-X.

Homer (adapted by Diana Stewart). **The Iliad.** Illus. Charles Shaw. 1981. ISBN 0-8172-1663-4.

Homer (adapted by Diana Stewart). **The Odyssey: Selected Adventures.** Illus. Konrad Hack. 1980. ISBN 0-8172-1654-5.

London, Jack (adapted by Lillian Nordlicht). **The Call of the Wild.** Illus. Juan Barberis. 1980. ISBN 0-8172-1656-1.

Poe, Edgar Allan (adapted by Diana Stewart). **Tales of Edgar Allan Poe.** Illus. Charles Shaw. 1981. ISBN 0-8172-1662-6.

Shakespeare, William (adapted by Diana Shaw). **Julius Caesar.** Illus. Charles Shaw. 1981. ISBN 0-8172-1664-2.

Shakespeare, William (adapted by Diana Stewart). **Romeo and Juliet.** Illus. Charles Shaw. 1980. ISBN 0-8172-1653-7.

Stevenson, Robert Louis (adapted by June Edwards). **Treasure Island.** Illus. Kinuko Craft. 1980. ISBN 0-8172-1655-3.

Twain, Mark (adapted by June Edwards). **Huckleberry Finn.** Illus. Sherry Neidigh. 1980. ISBN 0-8172-1651-0.

Twain, Mark (adapted by June Edwards). **Tom Sawyer.** Illus. Joel Naprstek. 1981. ISBN 0-8172-1665-0.

Verne, Jules (adapted by Lillian Nordlicht). **20,000 Leagues under the Sea.** Illus. Steve Butz. 1980. ISBN 0-8172-1652-9.

Raintree Machines Series

Spaceships, tugboats, amusement park rides, computers, submarines, racecars, and bulldozers—these are some of the machines described in this series. Photographs and drawings provide additional information. Raintree Childrens Books.

Ackins, Ralph. **Energy Machines.** 1980. ISBN 0-8172-1336-8.

Ciupik, Larry A., and James A. Seevers. **Space Machines.** 1979. ISBN 0-8172-1325-2.

Fenner, Sal. **Sea Machines.** 1980. ISBN 0-8172-1334-1.

Girard, Pat. **Flying Machines.** 1980. ISBN 0-8172-1333-3.

Hahn, Christine. **Amusement Park Machines.** 1979. ISBN 0-8172-1330-9.

Howard, Sam. **Communications Machines.** 1980. ISBN 0-8172-1335-X.

Kiley, Denise. **Biggest Machines.** 1980. ISBN 0-8172-1332-5.

Pick, Christopher C. **Oil Machines.** 1979. ISBN 0-8172-1327-9.

Pick, Christopher C. **Undersea Machines.** 1979. ISBN 0-8172-1326-0.

Stevens, Chris. **Fastest Machines.** 1980. ISBN 0-8172-1337-6.

Stone, William. **Earth Moving Machines.** 1979. ISBN 0-8172-1329-5.

Wykeham, Nicholas. **Farm Machines.** 1979. ISBN 0-8172-1328-7.

Random House Sports Library

George Brett, Larry Bird, Moses Malone, other sports heroes, and a few "goats" are featured in this series. Photographs show the sports stars in action. Random House.

Alfano, Pete. **Super Bowl Superstars: The Most Valuable Players in the NFL's Championship Game.** 1982. ISBN 0-394-85017-3.

Corn, Frederick Lynn. **Basketball's Magnificent Bird: The Larry Bird Story.** 1982. ISBN 0-394-85019-X (ISBN 0-394-95019-4, library binding).

Gergen, Joe. **World Series Heroes and Goats: the Men Who Made History in America's October Classic.** 1982. ISBN 0-394-85018-1 (ISBN 0-394-95018-6, library binding).

Hollander, Phyllis, and Zander Hollander, eds. **Touchdown! Football's Most Dramatic Scoring Feats.** 1982. ISBN 0-394-85020-3.

Hollander, Phyllis, and Zander Hollander, eds. **Winners under 21.** 1982. ISBN 0-394-85015-7 (ISBN 0-394-95015-1, library binding).

Twyman, Gib. **Born to Hit: The George Brett Story.** 1982. ISBN 0-394-85016-5 (ISBN 0-394-95016-X, library binding).

Sports Heroes Library

These sports books by Nathan Aaseng describe both superstars and great sports performances. Such sports as football, baseball, tennis, and soccer are discussed, and one book features athletes who overcame a handicap or misfortune to achieve greatness. Lerner Publications Co.

Football's Crushing Blockers. 1982. ISBN 0-8225-1074-X.
Football's Super Bowl Champions, I-VIII. 1982. ISBN 0-8225-1072-3.
Football's Super Bowl Champions, IX-XVI. 1982. ISBN 0-8225-1333-1.
Little Giants of Pro Sports. 1980. ISBN 0-8225-1059-6.
Memorable World Series Moments. 1982. ISBN 0-8225-1073-1.
Superstars Stopped Short. 1982. ISBN 0-8225-1326-9.
Winners Never Quit: Athletes Who Beat the Odds. 1980. ISBN 0-8225-1060-X.
Winning Women of Tennis. 1981. ISBN 0-8225-1067-7.

Triumph Series

Both fiction and nonfiction books make up this series. Fiction titles deal with disco and rock music and with suspense. The nonfiction books treat crime, the supernatural, and the recording industry. Bantam Books.

Atkinson, Linda. **Incredible Crimes.** 1981. ISBN 0-553-14938-5. Nonfiction.
Atkinson, Linda. **Psychic Stories Strange but True.** Illus. Marc Cohen. 1981. ISBN 0-553-14823-0. Nonfiction.
Dolan, Edward F., Jr. **The Bermuda Triangle and Other Mysteries of Nature.** 1981. ISBN 0-553-14824-9. Nonfiction. (A description of this book can be found in the Science section.)
Gathje, Curtis. **The Disco Kid.** Photographs by Carole Bertol. 1981. ISBN 0-553-14618-1. Fiction.
Rabinowich, Ellen. **Rock Fever.** Photographs by Mauro Marinelli. 1981. ISBN 0-553-14621-1. Fiction.
Thompson, Paul. **The Hitchhikers.** Photographs by Susan Kuklin. 1981. ISBN 0-553-14619-X. Fiction.
van Ryzin, Lani. **Cutting a Record in Nashville.** Photographs by author. 1981. ISBN 0-553-14620-3. Nonfiction.
White, Wallace. **One Dark Night.** Photographs by Bill Aron. 1981. ISBN 0-553-14822-2. Fiction.

Which Way Books

Jump into the world of fantasy, mystery, or the supernatural with this series. What happens in each book is decided by choices *you* make. R. G. Austin is the series author. Archway Paperbacks.

The Castle of No Return. Illus. Mike Eagle. 1982. ISBN 0-671-45756-4.

Curse of the Sunken Treasure. Illus. Lorna Tomei. 1982. ISBN 0-671-45098-0.

Famous and Rich. Illus. Mike Eagle. 1982. ISBN 0-671-43920-0.

Lost in a Strange Land. Illus. Lorna Tomei. 1982. ISBN 0-671-44110-8.

Vampires, Spies and Alien Beings. Illus. Anthony Kramer. 1982. ISBN 0-671-45758-6.

Afterword to the Teacher

As with previous editions, this booklist is designed for students who are able to read but who lack the motivation to do so because they have not encountered reading matter that speaks to their interests and concerns. As reluctant readers, these teenagers have yet to discover through print the pleasures of a well-conceived story, be it mystery, adventure, romance, or problem novel; the satisfaction of informative and interesting nonfiction; the delight of humor and poetry; the mind-stretching wonders of fantasy and science fiction; the chills of ghost and witch tales; the challenges of sports literature; the revelations of biography and autobiography; and the many other experiences that come through reading. Thus, in this new edition of *High Interest—Easy Reading* we offer a wide variety of recently published titles suitable in interest, quality, and ease of reading for capable but reluctant junior and senior high school students.

In selecting titles for inclusion, we have kept in mind the importance of a book's appeal in many dimensions: its title, its ability to grasp the reader's attention within a page or two, and its ability to carry the reader toward a satisfying conclusion or resolution while it employs a tone, style, and language that is engaging and honest and a format that is not demeaning or condescending. All titles included in this edition are new listings; most were published between 1979 and 1982. We do not include any works listed in prior editions of *High Interest—Easy Reading*, nor do we cite works frequently assigned as required reading. Those titles are already known to most teachers and media specialists.

The categories reflect careful deliberation on reader interest and appeal. One of the new features of this edition is in the inclusion of series books that have been carefully screened by the same standards we applied to individual listings; thus we excluded some titles in a series although they were published within the 1979–1982 time period. We agreed that a series book of special merit should, when appropriate, be included in another category as an individual listing. For example, we felt the Baker Street Irregulars mystery novels were so well done that we have listed them collectively in the Series category and individually in the Mystery and Crime category. The other Series books have a summary annotation for the entire series. Finally, the fact that we include in the Series section a number of adapted classics should not be taken as a blanket endorsement of such works. These particular titles do preserve the essence of the original work, while many adaptations do not.

We have not used the labels *Junior, Senior,* or *Junior/Senior* of prior editions. Instead, most fiction annotations indicate the age of the protagonist to give teachers and students some indication of the reading level of the intended audience. Because current young adult literature often displays aspects of realism that have become commonplace in much adult literature, we have included where appropriate a notice of mature language or subject matter. All books have been tested for readability, and none measure above an eighth-grade reading level.

Where we have been aware of titles available in both hard and soft cover, we have cited both. Full names and ordering addresses of publishers are listed in a Directory of Publishers at the end of the booklist. The International Standard Book Number (ISBN) listed in each book at the time of publication will help in the ordering process.

We sincerely hope this booklist will stimulate an interest in reading that will help students develop a more comfortable and rewarding relationship with books. We have read every title with care, have selected subjects of interest to high school students, and have applied suitable measures of readability to ensure that each book listed here is appropriate. We recommend this list to you and your students with best wishes for continued success in your reading program.

Hugh Agee
Editorial Chair

Directory of Publishers

Abingdon Press, Customer Service Dept., 201 Eighth Ave. S., Nashville, TN 37202

Aladdin Books. Imprint of Atheneum Publishers. Distributed by The Scribner Book Companies, 201 Willowbrook Blvd., Wayne, NJ 07470

Archway Paperbacks. Imprint of Pocket Books; division of Simon & Schuster, Inc. Orders to: Simon & Schuster, Inc., Total Warehouse Services, Radcliffe St., Bristol, PA 19007

Bantam Books, Inc. Orders to: 414 E. Golf Rd., Des Plaines, IL 60016

Benefic Press. Division of Coronado Publishers, Inc., 1250 Sixth Ave., San Diego, CA 92101

Camelot Books. Imprint of Avon Books, 959 Eighth Ave., New York, NY 10019

Carolrhoda Books, Inc., 241 First Ave. N., Minneapolis, MN 55401

Clarion Books. Imprint of Houghton Mifflin Co. Orders to: Houghton Mifflin Co., Wayside Rd., Burlington, MA 01803

Coward, McCann & Geoghegan, Inc., The Putnam Publishing Group. Orders to: One Grosset Dr., Kirkwood, NY 13795

Thomas Y. Crowell Co. Imprint of Harper & Row, Publishers, Inc. Orders to: Keystone Industrial Park, Scranton, PA 18512

Delacorte Press. Imprint of Dell Publishing Co., 1 Dag Hammarskjold Plaza, 245 E. 47th St., New York, NY 10017

André Deutsch Ltd. Distributed by E. P. Dutton, 2 Park Ave., New York, NY 10016

Dial Press, 1 Dag Hammarskjold Plaza, 245 E. 47th St., New York, NY 10017

Dodd, Mead & Co., 79 Madison Ave., New York, NY 10016

Doubleday & Co., Inc., 245 Park Ave., New York, NY 10167

E. P. Dutton, Inc., 2 Park Ave., New York, NY 10016

Elsevier/Nelson Books, 2 Park Ave., New York, NY 10016

M. Evans & Co., Inc. Distributed by E. P. Dutton, 2 Park Ave., New York, NY 10016

Flare Books. Imprint of Avon Books, 959 Eighth Ave., New York, NY 10019

Follett Publishing Co. Division of Follett Corp., 1010 W. Washington Blvd., Chicago, IL 60607

Four Winds Press. Imprint of Scholastic Book Services. Orders to: 906 Sylvan Ave., Englewood Cliffs, NJ 07632

Greenwillow Books. Division of William Morrow & Co., Inc. Orders to: William Morrow & Co., Inc., Wilmor Warehouse, 6 Henderson Dr., West Caldwell, NJ 07006

Harcourt Brace Jovanovich, Inc., 757 Third Ave., New York, NY 10017

Harper & Row, Publishers, Inc. Orders to: Keystone Industrial Park, Scranton, PA 18512

Hiway Books. Imprint of Westminster Press. Orders to: Order Dept., P.O. Box 718 Wm. Penn Annex, Philadelphia, PA 19105

Holiday House, Inc., 18 E. 53rd St., New York, NY 10022

Holt, Rinehart & Winston, Inc., 383 Madison Ave., New York, NY 10017

Houghton Mifflin Co. Orders to: Wayside Road, Burlington, MA 01803

Jem Books. Distributed by Julian Messner; division of Simon & Schuster, Inc. Orders to: Simon & Schuster, Inc., Total Warehouse Services Corp., Farragut Ave., Bristol, PA 19007

Alfred A. Knopf. Orders to: 400 Hahn Rd., Westminster, MD 21157

Landmark Books, Inc., 7847 12th Ave. S., Minneapolis, MN 55420

Laurel-Leaf Books. Imprint of Dell Publishing Co., Inc., 1 Dag Hammarskjold Plaza, 245 E. 47th St., New York, NY 10017

Lerner Publications Co., 241 First Ave., N., Minneapolis, MN 55401

J. B. Lippincott Co. Orders to: 2350 Virginia Ave., Hagerstown, MD 21740

Lodestar Books. Imprint of E. P. Dutton, 2 Park Ave., New York, NY 10016

Lothrop, Lee & Shepard Books. Division of William Morrow & Co., Inc., 105 Madison Ave., New York, NY 10016

Macmillan Publishing Co., Inc. Orders to: Front and Brown Sts., Riverside, NJ 08370

Julian Messner. Division of Simon & Schuster, Inc. Orders to: Simon & Schuster, Inc., Total Warehouse Services Corp., Farragut Ave., Bristol, PA 19007

William Morrow & Co., Inc., 105 Madison Ave., New York, NY 10016

Pantheon Books. Division of Random House, Inc. Orders to: Random House, Inc., 400 Hahn Rd., Westminster, MD 21157

Parnassus Press. Imprint of Houghton Mifflin Co. Orders to: Houghton Mifflin Co., Wayside Rd., Burlington, MA 01803

Pocket Books. Division of Simon & Schuster, Inc. Orders to: Simon & Schuster, Inc., Total Warehouse Services Corp., Farragut Ave., Bristol, PA 19007

G. P. Putnam's Sons, The Putnam Publishing Group. Orders to: 1050 Wall St. W., Lyndhurst, NJ 07071

Raintree Childrens Books. Imprint of Raintree Publishers Group. Orders to: Raintree Group Distribution Center, 424 N. Fourth St., 6th Floor, Milwaukee, WI 53203

Raintree Publishers Group. Orders to: Raintree Group Distribution Center, 424 N. Fourth St., 6th Floor, Milwaukee, WI 53203

Random House, Inc. Orders to: 400 Hahn Rd., Westminster, MD 21157

Charles Scribner's Sons. Orders to: Shipping and Service Center, Vreeland Ave., Totowa, NJ 07512

Seabury Press, Inc., 815 Second Ave., New York, NY 10017

Signet Books. Imprint of New American Library. Orders to: 120 Woodbine St., Bergenfield, NJ 07612

Signet Vista Books. Imprint of New American Library. Orders to: 120 Woodbine St., Bergenfield, NJ 07612

Skylight Books. Imprint of Dodd, Mead & Co., 79 Madison Ave., New York,
NY 10016

Sterling Publishing Co., Inc., 2 Park Ave., New York, NY 10016

Tempo Books. Imprint of The Berkley Publishing Group. Orders to: One
Commerce Rd., Pittston Township, PA 18640

Unicorn Books. Distributed by E. P. Dutton, 2 Park Ave., New York, NY 10016

Viking Press, Inc. Orders to: Viking/Penguin, Inc., 299 Murray Hill Pkwy.,
East Rutherford, NJ 07073

Westminster Press. Orders to: Order Dept., P.O. Box 718 Wm. Penn Annex,
Philadelphia, PA 19105

Albert Whitman & Co., 5747 W. Howard St., Niles, IL 60648

Author Index

Title Index